Is There Any Love Down Back?

The Four Boys

by

Alexander O'Neil

authorHOUSE™

1663 LIBERTY DRIVE, SUITE 200
BLOOMINGTON, INDIANA 47403
(800) 839-8640
WWW.AUTHORHOUSE.COM

First published by AuthorHouse 03/31/05

ISBN: 1-4208-4640-X (e)
ISBN: 1-4208-1706-X (sc)

Printed in the United States of America
Bloomington, Indiana

This book is printed on acid-free paper.

"Suffer little children, and forbid them not to come unto me."

MATTHEW 19:14

In Memory of Tony ("*The Bossy Cow*") R.I.P.

ACKNOWLEDGMENTS

I would like to first thank God up above for giving my brothers and me the strength to live through the traumas and pain that we endured. To those who had faith in me and encouraged me to write this book. I would like to say thanks to my "son" Keshawn Dodds and his lovely wife, Tammie, for their unconditional support and for giving me the inspiration to take on this project. I'd like to extend my appreciation to the "four boys," Trevon, Tahj, Marquis, and L. J., for helping me re-create the visual image of the four boys. I would like to thank Mark and Tina Cowles for their hospitality in allowing me to use their landscape to recreate the visual image of "Down Back." To Steve the "Greek" Marangoudakis for his help in my "Greek" oops! English literature. A special thank you to Ms. Willette Johnson, a high school principal who "corrected my manuscript"; she gave me an A, the first one I ever got. To my three children, Laurissa, Tanya, and Alex Jr. Last but not least a special thanks to my other half, "Liz." She has been there for me from the beginning. There were times that I was ready to quit writing and she would encourage me to continue on for my brothers and the "millions" of kids out there still in foster care.

There are a lot more people out there who have assisted me in this project. I sincerely appreciate all of the help that was given to me. **Thank you all!**

PROLOGUE

This book is dedicated to Tony, "the bossy cow," "the cowboy." (I know he is probably looking down on me, saying, "Make sure you tell like it was!") To my twin brother Arnold, my foster brother Michael, and all of the "kids" out there that are still in foster care.

This book is about the "four boys," Tony, Arnold, Michael, and me, placed in four different foster homes together. There were many reasons why we were placed in those homes. Each one of them had their share of traumas. We played together, cried together, laughed together, and suffered pain together. We comforted each other, we fought each other, we hated each other, and we loved each other. We had a camaraderie between us that would never be broken. We were—the four boys....

Somewhere over the rainbow way up high,

there's a land that I've heard of once in a lullaby."

Chapter 1

"The Beginning"

It was dark, very dark. There were few streetlights back then and even fewer in the country.

Looking across the road into the dark woods scared me to death as I sat on the front stairs outside by myself. I was so frightened that I was shivering and crying. I saw shiny green eyes staring back at me, I heard growls and grunts, and I just knew many dangerous wild animals, such as bears, wolves, foxes, even monsters, lived in those woods. I knew that one of them was going to come out of the woods and eat me up and nobody was going to be able to help me! I kept crying, wanting to go back into the house. I stood up and tried to open the door but I was too small and couldn't reach the doorknob, so I sat back down on the steps and cried. This was a form of punishment, meant to teach me a lesson, and I don't know what it was that I did to deserve this—I was four years old.

THE WHITMANS. OUR FIRST HOME 1948.

(Courtesy of Gloria May Peeler)

It was 1948. This is the year that Anthony "Tony" Gregory, my twin brother Arnold Barry O'Neil, Gary Allen "Michael" Gaulin, and myself were placed with the Massachusetts Department of Child Guardianship (D.C.G.), the state welfare. We four boys, as we were referred to by the Massachusetts State Welfare Department, were placed together with our first set of foster parents in Richmond, Massachusetts. Arnold and I were born in East Lyme, Connecticut. We lost our mother to tuberculosis in 1948. Tony was born in Tewksbury, Massachusetts. It is unknown who or where his parents are.

Michael was born in Springfield, Massachusetts. He was seriously injured in a bad car accident with his first set of foster parents in Lee, Massachusetts, November 26, 1948. His foster father was arrested for drunk driving; consequently Michael was taken from that foster home and placed with us. He was two years old at the time of the accident.

Our foster parents were Virgil and Patricia Gertrude Whitman. Virgil was a big man, about six feet tall, light complexioned, with one eye missing. Patricia Whitman was a small woman who stood about four feet tall. She was dark complexioned and wore thick glasses. We had to call her "Miss Patty."

There were six other foster kids already staying at the Whitmans before our arrival. There was Gloria May, her sister Delores, and their four brothers Ronnie, Herbie, Lloyd, and Walter. This was the first foster home that I remember. My state records showed that Arnold and myself spent the first three years of our lives in foster care in Cambridge, Massachusetts. At the age of four we were placed with the other kids in Richmond, Massachusetts. This home was a big farm with a huge eight-room house on the land, a barn, and a lot of farm animals: horses, cows, pigs, and millions of chickens. Here there were acres and acres of farmland, beautifully landscaped, with mountains and valleys with fresh-water streams flowing right out of the mountains. This was the Berkshires. People come here every summer. It was a hunters' Shangri-la; folks went there just to get away. This was a paradise for a lot of people, but for the four boys it was a living hell.

I don't remember too much about the Whitmans, although there is one incident that stands out in my mind that's rather humorous. Miss Patty used to sing a church song called "Heavenly Sunshine" and oftentimes when she got in the mood to sing it, she would have Arnold and myself sing along with her. It must have paid off.

One day Miss Patty decided to take some ferns to the market in Pittsfield, Massachusetts. While she was driving, she started singing and had Arnold and me sing along with her. Suddenly she bent over to make an adjustment on the passenger-side window, and in doing so she lost control of the car. It started rolling down an embankment into a ditch. We were screaming and crying; fortunately, none of us was hurt. After a brief struggle with the steering wheel, "Miss Patty" managed to get the car back on the dirt road. You can best believe that after that we all sang a little louder! Somebody was watching over us.

At first it seemed that Miss Patty cared a lot for Arnold and me. She spent a lot of time with us, taking us to the store with her and to the market in Pittsfield. We were only four years old at the time. She was proud of "her two little twins." She took us everywhere at first—then things started to change. I think she was getting tired of us and her patience was beginning to wear. She started finding reasons to punish us and beat us with her leather strap. I guess it wasn't easy taking care of ten kids, but since there was a shortage of *colored* foster homes we were all stuck here together. "Miss Patty" didn't treat Arnold and me as meanly as she did Gloria and her brothers.

Tony had a bad habit of "messing" in his pants. I remember on one occasion when Tony soiled his pants, Miss Patty became furious and made him take off the soiled underwear. Once he had them removed, Miss Patty snatched them from him and wiped them across his face, smearing "doo,doo" all over his face like paint and shouting in a loud voice at him, telling him that "this ought to teach you a lesson" and "you better start learning how to use the bathroom." She was screaming real loud at Tony, her body was shaking, and she was sweating. It seemed like she was having a fit of some sort. Tony was seven years old, and as she was reprimanding him he began to cry. Miss Patty screamed at him to be quiet or else she was going to beat him. You could smell the feces that was on his face, and when he started crying, some of it got into his mouth. He spit it out and continued to cry. Miss Patty continued to yell at Tony. She then grabbed him by the arm and marched him outside to the front of the house, where she pushed him down on the front steps and told him to sit there until he learned to go to the bathroom. Tony sat outside on the steps crying with feces all over his face; all he had on was a T-shirt, with nothing on his bottom except "doo-doo" stains. We could hear Tony outside crying and the rest of us started crying too. Miss Patty told us to "button up" or we would get the same thing. She then made us all go to bed, all except Tony. The rest of us went upstairs to our bedroom whimpering. We were afraid that she was going to beat us too, or make us sit on the steps outside in the dark. It seemed like a long time before she brought little Tony back inside the house. When she did he was still whimpering; she told him to get upstairs to bed.

Sitting on the steps outside or inside, depending on what type of mood Miss Patty was in, was a routine punishment for us if we misbehaved. Sometimes we were forced to sit on the steps for hours at a time. There were a lot of woods across the street from where we lived and Miss Patty knew that we were afraid to sit outside by ourselves at night. I always preferred the inside steps myself; at least it was safe. I knew that the animals in the woods wouldn't come in the house and eat me up.

One morning while we were eating breakfast, which was a bowl of pabulum, Miss Patty was attempting to feed little Michael his pabulum but he kept pushing it away. Pabulum was a creamy cereal similar to oatmeal; it didn't taste too bad; however, Michael didn't like it and he decided that he was not going to eat it! Miss Patty was becoming very irritable with Michael. He had his mind made up that he was not going to eat pabulum today, period! Once again Miss Patty tried to feed him. And again Michael pushed the spoon away. That was the last straw. Miss Patty hauled off and slapped him in the face. Poor little Michael jerked his head back in shock and pain and started crying as loud as he could. Miss Patty went over to the sink and dumped the pabulum in it and walked away, leaving Michael still crying. She turned and pointed her finger at him telling him to be quiet, and that if he had eaten his pabulum this never would have happened. Michael cried harder and louder. This agitated Miss Patty and she walked over to him and raised her hand and slapped him in the face again, screaming for him to "shut up." She snatched him out of his high chair and started shaking him, trying to make him be quiet. Virgil came into the kitchen and asked her what was going on. She said, "This boy ain't eatin' his food and I slapped him, and if he doesn't shut up I will smack him again." She was holding Michael by the arm with him hanging down by her side crying. The rest of us were sitting at the table eating our pabulum. We felt sorry for little Michael. Finally Miss Patty put him back in his high chair and walked away mumbling to herself about how sorry she was for taking us in—we were sorry too! At that time Michael was three years old.

Virgil Whitman, our "father," was no saint either. He was a strange man. Sometimes he was even scary-looking with his one eye, and he never smiled. Some days he would be in a good mood and others in a bad one. There were times he would take us to ball games. I remember one day while we were riding in his truck he took Arnold in his lap, showing him how to steer the car. At times he actually acted like a father, but that was rare. His favorite thing was chasing us around the yard with dead snakes. He loved doing that. He knew that we were scared to death of the dead snakes, and when he really got into it he would chase us around the yard whirling a dead snake like a rope in the air then throw it at us leaving us screaming and frantically running around the yard. He thought that it was hilarious. We didn't.

Virgil was a cook at a local boarding school. Oftentimes he would bring home some leftover food that tasted like garbage, which is probably what it was. He forced us to eat it or else. He was a lousy cook. I guess because the people that he worked for didn't eat it, he felt that since he was the cook somebody had to eat it. He wasn't about to throw his hard work away!

VIRGIL'S BARN -FILE-DWNBK-E"

(Courtesy of Gloria May Peeler)

Virgil Whitman had a habit of taking Gloria and her sister Deloris out to the barn in the rear of the house and sexually molesting them. Virgil would force both Gloria and her sister Delores to go to the barn, and then he would have one of them stand outside by the door so that no one would walk in on him. And he would take the other inside and force her to perform oral sex on him and fondle his genitals. At that time Gloria was only seven years old and Delores was six.

As we got older "our parents" gave us chores to do. We had more chores than the average child should have; chores such as cleaning out the barn, feeding the pigs, cleaning out the pig pen, and going into the woods and pulling up ferns. Miss Patty used to sell the ferns at a market in Pittsfield. One of the chores that were assigned to us was plucking the dead chickens that the Whitmans sold at the market in Pittsfield. Plucking a chicken means pulling all of the feathers off of it before sending it to the market to be sold. It was a time-consuming task. Most of the time it was the older kids like Herbie, Walter, and Gloria who had to do it. One day when Virgil was in the kitchen washing the chickens that Herbie and the other kids had previously plucked, Tony walked up to him feeling proud as a peacock because he had plucked all of the feathers off of his chicken; but apparently he didn't get all of the feathers off, because when he handed Virgil the chicken, Virgil looked at it and flew into a rage, tossing the half-plucked chicken on the floor, shouting at Tony, telling him that the chicken still had feathers on it. Poor Tony, feeling dejected, turned and walked back to the chicken coop with his half-plucked chicken hanging down by his side. Gloria saw him returning back to the chicken coop with his chicken and asked him what happened. Tony said, "Daddy hollered at me."

At least once each day, one of us would get a beating with a leather belt that Miss Patty had. It was a homemade belt with strips of leather tied together. When she used it, believe me, it hurt. One day right after a heavy rainstorm, Arnold and I were standing in a mud puddle stomping and splashing water on each other like two little nuts, getting our clothes wet and dirty. Miss Patty came outside and saw us and became infuriated. She told us to "get in the house right now!" I was scared because I knew that we were going to get a beating. Miss Patty shouted at us, saying, "How many times do I have to tell you about playing in the water, huh? I tell you time after time and you want to be hard headed. Well, maybe this will teach you a lesson." I started crying before she even started the whipping. I begged her, "Please don't beat me. I'm sorry. I won't do it no more!"

Arnold and Alex—Richmond Mass 1948

(Courtesy of Gloria May Peeler)

Miss Patty had her mind made up and that was that! She took the leather belt and started beating both Arnold and me with it. Miss Patty kept beating us and telling us that we were hard headed, and this is what we were going to get each time we misbehaved. She shouted for us to be quiet. Arnold stopped crying but I kept on, and this made Miss Patty angrier. She picked me up and started shaking me, shouting at me, telling me to be quiet, but I still kept crying. She slammed me against the wall causing my head to bang against it, and then dropped me on the floor, which made me cry even harder. Gloria was in the kitchen washing dishes. When she saw what Miss Patty was doing to me she began to cry too. Miss Patty looked at her and said, "Oh you want to cry too? Well, I'll give you something to cry about!" She then walked over to where Gloria was and started whipping her with the leather belt. Poor Gloria got a whipping for feeling sorry for me. From that day on I began to have bad headaches that continue to this day.

Miss Patty used to always beat Lloyd and Gloria for trivial things that they did. Sometimes she would force Gloria, her sister, and brothers to beat themselves and each other. If Miss Patty didn't think that they were beating each other hard enough she would do it.

I remember Gloria telling me that one day when she and her sister Dolores were arguing over who was supposed to wash dishes, Miss Patty took them both outside and tied them to a tree in the woods and left them there for hours. She said that it was about 4:00 p.m. when she took them out to the tree and about 1:00 a.m. when Miss Patty came back out to get them. She must have forgotten all about them. It was dark and cold and Gloria said that they were both very afraid.

Virgil had a gun that he kept in the house. It was an old .22 rifle that he used to shoot the wild animals that would stalk his henhouse. One day while he and Patty were off to the market, Tony found the gun and started playing cowboys with it. Suddenly it went off, shooting a hole into the floor. Thank God he didn't point the gun at one of us. Tony became scared and told us not tell on him. We promised that we wouldn't. He then found some black electrical tape and covered up the hole with it.

I was lying in the bed that day sick with a cold, and when Virgil Whitman came home I crawled out of my bed and pointed to the hole in the floor and shouted, "Bullet! Bullet!" Virgil found the hole in the floor and asked what had happened. He asked me, "Who did that?" I pointed at Tony and said he did it. Virgil turned and looked at Tony and asked him if he was playing with his gun and did he shoot the hole in the floor. Tony hesitated for a moment and held his head down and whispered, "Yes, Daddy, but I'm sorry. I won't do it no more." Virgil took off his leather belt and told Tony to go to his room. We could hear him beating Tony and telling him never to touch his gun again. After it was over Tony came out of his room with tears in his eyes, giving me a real dirty look. That look he gave me told me that if he ever got his hands on the rifle again, or any gun for that matter, it wouldn't be the floor that he would put a bullet in!

I remember one day Virgil took Arnold and me to a baseball game. It was real hot and I was suffering from another one of my bad headaches. I told Virgil that I had a headache but he ignored me and continued to watch the game. The pain was excruciating. Arnold tried to comfort me. I kept crying because my head was hurting real bad. Virgil told me to shut up and be quiet and watch the game, and that if I sat still my headache would go away. Well, it didn't. It was hurting real bad. My head was hurting so bad I was getting dizzy. I felt like vomiting. Virgil was so into the baseball game that he didn't care about my headache. When I got back home I told Miss Patty that I had a bad headache. She gave me a pill and sent me to bed. To this day I hate going to baseball games. I don't even watch them on TV.

One day while Gloria and her sister Delores were outside playing in the yard, her little brother Herbie came out crying and holding his ear. It looked like it was bleeding. Gloria asked him, "What happened?"

He said, "Momma spanked me."

Just then Miss Patty came out and heard what he said. She told him if he didn't shut up she would beat him again, and that he better not ever tell the "state man." The state man was the D.C.G. social worker that periodically came to visit us and check on our well-being.

Well, somebody told the state man something, because Gloria and her brothers were finally removed from the Whitmans. Gloria told me that not long after when she and her brothers were placed in a home in Springfield, Massachusetts, that she reported to the D.C.G. the sexual abuse that took place in the barn by Virgil Whitman in Richmond as well as a few other things that he did.

Eventually Virgil was arrested and sent to jail, leaving Miss Patty to look after us by herself for a year. She pleaded with the D.C.G. to have us removed prior to Virgil's release from the institution, for fear of him retaliating against us for what happened to him. The State Welfare

Department frantically searched for a *colored* foster home to place us in so that we would be gone when Virgil was released from prison.

The Massachusetts Welfare Department finally found another colored foster home for the four boys; our new home was in Pittsfield, Massachusetts.

It was 1952.

Chapter 2

"Down Back"

"Get your behind upstairs to bed right now, you ain't gettin' no supper, you hear me?"

Once again poor Arnold would get sent to bed on an empty stomach and he would cry himself to sleep.

This was Pittsfield, Massachusetts, 1952.

Pittsfield, Massachusetts, is a quiet little town in the "Berkshires," a mountain range located in the northwestern part of New England. We lived on Cole Avenue, way up on the hill, in the last house on the street, Arnold, Michael, Tony, and me: the "four boys." This is where we spent the next five years of our lives in misery.

Our foster parents were Charles Edmonds ("Uncle Charlie," as he wanted to be called) and Hazel Edmonds. Uncle Charlie was short and stocky. His eyes were small and sunk in and his nose kind of reminded me of a rooster because it was long and pointed. Hazel Edmonds demanded to be called "Mrs. Edmonds" every time we addressed her. It was always, "Yes, Mrs. Edmonds," "No, Mrs. Edmonds." It got to the point that when we spoke to her, it came out like, "Yes, Miz Edmonds," "No, Miz Edmonds," especially when we were anticipating a beating, or became excited about something. Mrs. Edmonds was small in stature and light complexioned. Any time we spoke with either of the Edmondses we had to hold our heads down. We could not look them in the face. The Edmondses had five children of their own, "Billie," Chuck, Thomas, who lived next door to us, Herbert, a sixteen-year-old "bully," whom they called Herbie for short, and an older daughter named Edith. Edith was big as a house and worked in a hospital. She had a daughter named Patricia, or "Patsy," as we called her. Herbie, Edith, and Patsy lived in the same house with us.

Uncle Charlie managed a charcoal business called the New England Carbon Works. It was a large kiln set back in the fields. This is where they made and packed charcoal briquettes for sale. Oftentimes Uncle Charlie would take all four of us to the kiln to help him pack the small charcoal briquettes in boxes that he prepared for sale. We never saw anybody else working at the kiln. I remember the smell was awful, the soot was thick, and every time we coughed, thick soot would come up from our lungs. There was charcoal dust everywhere; the air was thick with it. Quite often Uncle Charlie would take Arnold to the kiln alone. The rest of us used to get jealous, thinking that Uncle Charlie favored Arnold more than the rest of us.

Herbie the "bully" had a bad habit of picking on Arnold and me. He would use Arnold and me as punching bags. Herbie would come up to our bedroom and start playfully punching us. But each time he punched us the punches would get harder and harder. He enjoyed doing that to us. I guess he got off on doing that. We kept telling him that he was hurting us, but he just laughed and continued to pound on us. Eventually he would stop banging on us and run back downstairs singing his favorite song, "Earth Angel," leaving Arnold and me in pain.

One evening while Arnold and I were getting ready for bed, Herbie came to our room and went over to Arnold and told him to close his eyes and open his mouth. When Arnold did as he was told, Herbie took out his penis and put it in Arnold's mouth and laughed, saying, "Suck my c##k." Arnold jerked his head back gagging! Herbie put is penis back in his pants and ran downstairs laughing hysterically. Every day when Herbie got bored, he would find some way to pick on one of us. There were times he would pick little Michael up off of the ground and slam him back down with extreme force, causing Michael to cry in pain. He very seldom bothered Tony. He had a bad habit of sneaking up on Arnold and me at any given time and banging our heads together real hard. So hard I would see stars and hear a ringing in my ears. He thought that was hilarious. When Herbie did that on one of my headache days it would hurt real bad. There were times when Herbie would be bored, and after he had had a few beers he would blast the radio in his 1955 Chevrolet listening to the do-wop station. And as soon as his favorite song, "Earth Angel," came on he would start singing out loud and dare us to laugh at him. He sounded awful but none of us dared laugh at him, much as we wanted to.

All four of us slept in the same room on the second floor (two to a bed). In the earlier years, all of us had a bad habit of wetting the bed. Each morning Mrs. Edmonds would check to see if our beds were wet. When she found one she would fly into a rage and ask which one of us wet the bed. The guilty one would confess and she would make him strip, then beat the crap out of him with a flat board that she always used.

Second foster home, Pittsfield, Massachusetts

(Courtesy A. R. O'Neil)

The landscape around the Edmondses' house was beautiful. There was a big flower garden located on the south side of the yard where they held their annual family picnic. In the rear of the house was a large wooded area. This is where the Edmondses called "down back." Down back is where we were confined. We were not allowed to enter the house under any circumstances without permission. If we had to use the bathroom we had to knock on the door before going in the house. Most of the time we went behind a tree and pee-peed. Whenever one of us had to "doo-doo" we went to the house and knocked on the door. Either Edith or Mrs. Edmonds would answer and in a mean voice ask, "What do you want now?"

I would say, "I'm sorry Miz Edmonds but I have to "doo-doo."

She would then point upstairs and say, "Get up there and hurry up, and you better not mess in your clothes—now get going!" Otherwise we did most of our body flushing outside in the woods.

The winter months in the Berkshires were brutal. There were times when we had to walk to school in near-blizzard conditions. The snow would be up to our waists and it would be brutally cold with the wind blowing in our faces. No one wanted to give us a ride as we trudged along in the deep snow. We saw other kids riding in cars with their parents, and as they passed by us we were hoping that they would stop and offer us a ride. But then who would stop and give four *colored* boys a ride? We had to brave the cold and do the best that we could, all four of us, with Tony in the lead. Michael could hardly keep up with the rest of us. The snow was almost up to his neck. After school we were forced to stay outside in the woods. "Down back" in the cold, for hours, we were not allowed to go inside the house to get warm. We were forced to stay outside until Mrs. Edmonds banged on the kitchen window. That was the traditional signal for us to come into the house to eat. We were dressed in skimpy clothes, which consisted of thin mittens, buckle-up boots, and thin overcoats. Many days we would suffer from minor frostbite on our hands and feet.

On those cold days when there was no school and we were "put outside," none of us was in a mood to play because of the cold. Tony would have us marching around in a little circle to keep warm. We used to walk around and around with our heads down. It would be so cold. With the wind blowing and flurries hitting us in the face, poor little Michael used to cry because he was the youngest. He was only six years old and he suffered the most. Tony would yell at Michael and tell him to stop whining. I think it was just out of frustration, because he couldn't do anything to help him. More than once Tony would go to the house and ask for permission for us to come inside but was always refused. He would get shouted at by Mrs. Edmonds and told to get his butt back "down back," telling him that she would let us know when it was time to come inside and not before. So we marched around and around, shivering from the cold; our feet would be numb. I felt sorry for little Michael. We were all freezing. We kept staring at the window, praying for that knock. Finally Mrs. Edmonds would knock on the window and yell to us to come inside and "get this or I will throw it away," meaning our supper. She would tell us this every time that she knocked on the window. Every now and then she would give her granddaughter Patsy the honor of knocking on the window. We would then ceremoniously file into the house and sit on the floor and thaw out. Rusty, their pet collie, would already be stretched out on the floor under the table, nice and warm. He was treated better than we were. We were not allowed to sit at the table until it was time to eat. Every time we entered the house it was mandatory that we sit on the floor in a small pantry space near the kitchen.

Some of those cold days were not too bad. In the morning and into the late afternoon it would be somewhat warm, and we would build snowmen and snow forts. We bombarded each other with snowballs, making the most out of the day. When evening came the temperature would drop and it would start getting colder. The snowballing would stop and we found ourselves again marching around in our circle, with Tony in front leading the way.

"Down back" is where we found ourselves every day after school. There we would sit on an old discarded hot water heater and talk about what had happened in school that day. Tony would tell us how much he hated school and that some day he was going to run away. The rest of us dared not to even think of running away.

Chapter 3

"Hunger Pains"

For some reason, which we couldn't understand, Mrs. Edmonds picked on Arnold more than the rest of us. She would always find a reason to send him to bed without supper. At times she would give him a slice of bread with gravy with a glass of water. We would all be sitting at the dinner table with our meals, and Arnold would have a slice of bread with gravy on it on his plate and nothing more. She would do that to Arnold two or three times a month.

Whenever Arnold was sent to bed without supper we would sneak food up to him. Most of the time Tony, the bold one, would volunteer to do it. He would put scraps of food in his pockets and then ask permission to use the bathroom upstairs. He would then dash up the stairs and slip into the bedroom where Arnold was and hand him the food scraps from of his pockets. Arnold would sit up in the bed and devour the small pieces of chicken or hamburger or whatever Tony brought up to him. After Tony slipped Arnold the food scraps, he would then go into the bathroom and flush the toilet as if he used it and come back downstairs. Oftentimes the type of food that we had we couldn't put in our pockets to sneak up to him, such as spaghetti or homemade baked beans. Those were the times that he had to go without. Arnold would cry his eyes out but the adults did not hear him, and no one except us cared. Every now and then another one of us would volunteer to go on the rescue mission so the Edmondses didn't get suspicious. We felt that Mrs. Edmonds would catch on if Tony kept asking to use the bathroom every time she sent Arnold to bed without supper. I was too chicken to do it, so I waited until bedtime, and then I would give Arnold the food out of my pockets. Arnold would really *starve* to death waiting on me if I was the only one that he depended on. Thank God none of us ever got caught. I have to admit our pants pockets got kind of messy at times. I'm surprised Mrs. Edmonds didn't catch on just from the greasy pockets on our jeans.

Often times when all four of us would be sitting at the table eating our meals, Arnold and Tony would take food off of Michael's and my plate. They knew that we couldn't do anything because we were smaller than them. We all used to sit at the table with our arms circling our plates in a protective manner. But that didn't stop Tony or Arnold; if they wanted more food they would take some of Michael's or mine and dare us to tell on them. They knew that we would get mad at them but they didn't care.

I used to try to eat my food as fast as I could before they could get to my plate. I damn near choked myself to death many times in an attempt to eat as much food as I could off my plate before Arnold or Tony got to it.

Tony was bold and brash. We all looked up to him as our leader, the "boss." "The bossy cow" we called him. Always after dinner we would go back to the pantry area and sit on the floor and whisper among ourselves about how mean Mrs. Edmonds was and how "kind" Uncle Charlie was to us, and how nice he was to Arnold and how nice it would be if we could just go to another foster home. Tony said one day if he ever got the nerve he would run away and tell somebody about the Edmondses. He said more than likely no one would pay any attention to him but he was going to try anyway.

Tony knew how to make us feel safe and comfortable at times like these. He was the oldest of the four boys. After about an hour or so, we were sent to bed. Arnold would already be in bed asleep, his pillow still wet from crying. Arnold cried himself to sleep on an empty stomach quite often. Some nights he would have something in his stomach, thanks to Tony.

Oftentimes Arnold would be weak and dizzy from the lack of food. There were times that we would be so hungry we would pick clovers, berries, and rotten apples. Arnold used to climb the apple trees and pick rotten apples and throw them down to us to eat. We used to sneak into the Edmondses' garden and steal the tomatoes and raw onions out of it. They also had a rhubarb patch behind the house. It tasted awful raw but it was better than nothing. Luckily we never got caught stealing the vegetables from the Edmonds garden. Whatever we ate, we pretended it was our supper, while waiting for the traditional knock on the window so we could go inside and eat a real meal.

There were days that Mrs. Edmonds would send us to school hungry. Our breakfast consisted of cold cereal with little or no milk; it was just as if we had had no breakfast at all. Many times while we were on the way to school we would dig into garbage cans looking for something to eat. We would go from one end of the street to the other and look into each can for food scraps to eat. At the time it seemed like the natural thing to do; we didn't give it a second thought. It became a habit with us because we were always hungry. The residents on Cole Avenue would look out of their windows early in the morning and see four colored boys digging through their garbage cans. We used to look for discarded candy and pastries; anything that we thought was edible. Often we would find discarded loaves of bread with mold on the crust. We would scrap off the moldy crust and eat the inside of the bread. At supper and if we all got the opportunity to eat, we were not allowed to ask for seconds. That's when Arnold and Tony attacked Michael's and my plates. Many times we would leave the dinner table still hungry and go to bed on half-empty stomachs. The garbage cans were an opportunity to put food in our stomachs, along with the "stuff" that we stole from the local stores. Every now and then someone would see us rummaging through their garbage and feel sorry for us. They would come out and give us fruits or food scraps. One day while we were scavenging through a garbage can, an old lady came out and asked us what we were doing. We told her that we were hungry and we were just looking for something to eat. I could have sworn that I saw tears in her eyes as she turned and went back into the house. A couple of minutes later she came back out and handed us a huge Hershey chocolate and almond bar. We split it up and, of course, Tony got the biggest piece. We thanked her and she stepped briskly back into the house. Farther on down the street, another lady came out and asked us what were we looking for in her garbage can, and didn't we know any better then to dig in people's trash? We told her that we were looking for food to eat. She asked us where we lived. We told her and she then went back inside the house. Some of the cans we came across were filled with maggots. Those cans we passed by. We would be disappointed when we came up empty handed. That's when Tony or Arnold would go to a house and knock on the door, asking for something to eat. The rest of us would just stand on the sidewalk watching, looking pitiful! A lot of people on our street had fruit trees in their backyard: apples, pears, peaches, and even a few grape vines. Every now and then we would make a mad dash into a backyard and grab some apples or pears to munch on, on the way to school. Sometimes we would get caught and chased out of the yards, or somebody's dog would have fun chasing us out.

As time went on, Tony was getting older and becoming more aggressive and harder to control. The first time he ran away we thought that he ran away to find somebody to tell about our dilemma. Tony ran away about two or three times while we were at the Edmondses, and each time the D.C.G. brought him back to the Edmondses. Each time after the state people brought Tony back he would get the beating of his life. Mrs. Edmonds showed him no mercy. She used her famous board to do it with, then after the beating she would send him up to his room without supper. The rest of us plotted on who was going to sneak food up to him. Tony told us more than once that whenever he was sent to bed without supper that he didn't want any of us to sneak food up to him. I think it was a pride thing with him, but we still used to do it anyway, and when we did, Mr. Pride would gobble it up and say thanks in his Western drawl then roll over and pretend that he was going to sleep. In actuality he was hiding the tears in his eyes from us; we all knew that.

Each time Tony ran away and got caught we would ask him where did he go and what did he do? He would say that he went downtown trying to find the state people to tell them about the Edmondses. We knew that he was lying because we heard the state people tell Mrs. Edmonds that Tony was found in a store stealing candy and pastries.

When Tony took off on us, we would be angry with him because we felt that he had abandoned us. We thought that maybe he would get put in jail and we would never see him again. He had his rotten ways about him, but we felt that we could not live without him. We used to call him "the bossy cow." Only God knows how we came up with a nickname like that, but it stuck. Each time we called him that he would get mad at us. Tony always wanted to be a cowboy like John Wayne and boss us around, so we called him "the bossy cow" and left the "boy" out; that's the part that he didn't like I guess. He told us that each time he was caught by the child guidance people he would try to tell them what was going on but they didn't seem to care. They figured that Tony was lying just to keep from getting punished for running away, or maybe they could care less. After all we were just four colored boys in a colored foster home, and they were far and few between! Finding another one that would take in four boys was almost impossible.

Chapter 4
"I'm sorry, Miz Edmonds, I won't do it no more"

Every summer in the month of August, the Edmondses held their family picnic. They would host a large gathering of family and friends. We used to sit in the woods and watch everybody have a good time. We asked if we could come out and play with the other kids but Mrs. Edmonds flatly refused to let us join the family festivities. I guess she thought that we weren't good enough to be part of the family picnic. We watched Patsy and her little cousins chase each other across the yard, playing tag. Every so often they would stop in front of the woods where we were, and Patsy would point at us and say something smart then they would all start giggling and run off. Herbie would be sitting in the garden with his white friends, drinking beer and listening to his doo-wop music. Every so often he would look over at us and say something to his friends. And they would all start chuckling. Uncle Charlie was in his glory. He was Mr. Chef Boyardee doing his thing on the grill: hot dogs, hamburgers, steaks, shish kebabs, homemade baked beans, barbecue ribs—you name it, they had it. All we could do was watch and smell the food that was being cooked. Later in the evening when everybody was gone, Miz Edmonds ordered us to clean up the mess that everybody made. That's when we had our little picnic. We found half-eaten hot dogs and hamburgers along with half-eaten corn on the cob still on the paper plates on the table. So as we cleaned we ate the leftovers.

Uncle Charlie Edmonds came outside one day and called Arnold to the house; I guess he wanted Arnold to help him out at the charcoal kiln. Arnold slowly walked out of the woods with Uncle Charlie and both of them got in the car and drove off. Arnold didn't look too happy. I didn't know why. An hour or so later they came back and Arnold went off in another part of the woods and sat down. He had a strange look on his face. We couldn't figure out what was wrong with him. After all, Uncle Charlie favored him more than the rest of us and we did not like that. Maybe that was what was wrong with Arnold; maybe he thought we were mad at him because he was Uncle Charlie's favorite. After a while Arnold came over to where we were and started playing with us as if nothing ever happened.

It was very seldom that Uncle Charlie raised his voice at us, and when he did it was because we did something real bad. He was very soft-spoken. For some reason he seemed to treat us better than Mrs. Edmonds did. I think sometimes he would feel sorry for the way Miz Edmonds treated us. I remember one hot summer day while we doing our chores and helping Uncle Charlie with yard work, we heard the familiar sound of the ice cream truck with its bells ringing coming down the street. Uncle Charlie gave each of us a quarter for a popsicle. He then went into the house, but before the truck came up to the house Mrs. Edmonds, who must have been looking out of the window and saw Uncle Charlie give us the money, came outside and made us give her the quarters that Uncle Charlie gave us. We reluctantly gave them to her and she scurried back into the house. The ice cream truck slowly drove past our house with its bells ringing, and all four of us just stood there watching the other kids running up to it to get their popsicles and ice cream. We turned and walked back down back; a short time later Uncle Charlie came back out and asked us if we got popsicles. We told him that Mrs. Edmonds took the quarters that he gave us. He said he would talk to her about that; he didn't know why she did it. So that was that. We spent the rest of the day finishing up our chores. Uncle Charlie liked Arnold a lot. On the other hand, Mrs. Edmonds seemed to have an enormous dislike for Arnold and me.

There were times that Arnold would not come straight home after school. We would wait for him outside after school but Arnold was nowhere to be found. So we would start walking home without him. I think most of the time he just didn't want to go home, knowing that Mrs. Edmonds would find some reason to beat him or send him to bed without his supper. Oftentimes he would wander off into stores in downtown Pittsfield, and other times he would go into people's yards taking fruit from their trees.

One day when Arnold was late coming home, the rest of us were down back wondering what happened to him. Tony said he probably ran away. Suddenly, as we looked up there was Arnold with an older white lady, walking up the driveway. The lady knocked on the door, and when Mrs. Edmonds answered it, the white lady said that she found Arnold in her backyard stealing pears from her trees, and when she asked him why was he stealing her pears he told her that he was hungry. Mrs. Edmonds told the lady that Arnold had no reason to be hungry; he got plenty of food to eat. We knew that she was lying, but the white lady didn't. Mrs. Edmonds said he just wanted to take something to see if he could get away with it. "I'll take care of it from here. Thank you for bringing him home." The lady then turned and walked away. Mrs. Edmonds told Arnold to go to his room. The rest of us knew what was going to happen next. It seemed like Arnold asked for the beatings from Mrs. Edmonds. He knew that if he got caught stealing or if he was late coming home he would get a beating with the board.

Another day when Arnold was late coming home from school, the rest of us had already changed our clothes and started our chores. When Arnold finally got home, Mrs. Edmonds told him to go upstairs to his room. We all knew that he was going to get another beating. We felt bad for him. We could hear him telling Miz Edmonds that he was sorry for being late again. Miz Edmonds had her mind made up. She told Arnold to take off his clothes. When he did she made him bend over the back of a chair.

Arnold kept begging her not to beat him, telling her that he was sorry and that he "wouldn't do it no more." It was no use; Mrs.

Edmonds continued to whip him with the wooden paddle. She was hitting Arnold so hard we could hear it all the way outside, along with his screaming. She yelled at him, telling him, "I hope this will teach you a lesson. I'm tired of you coming home late from school all the time. I'm the boss here, and when I say be home at a certain time I mean it. Do you understand me?"

"Yes, Miz Edmonds, please don't hit me no more."

The three of us sat in the woods in silence, listening, and feeling the pain. Michael had tears in his eyes and Tony just sat there with a stony look on his face. Finally after what seemed like an eternity, Mrs. Edmonds stopped beating Arnold. We thought that she would send him back down back with us, but instead she sent him to bed. It was about 3:00 in the evening. Poor Arnold had to stay in his room the rest of the day. He wasn't allowed to come out except to use the bathroom. Once again we snuck food up to him at bedtime. Arnold was still crying when we went to bed that night. He couldn't lie on his back because his buttocks were raw from the beating that Mrs. Edmonds gave him Uncle Charlie was nowhere to be found. Herbie thought it was funny every time one of us got a beating. I can't ever recall seeing Herbie get scolded or beaten.

As time went on and as he got older, Michael started taking things from school. One day the principal at Redfield School called Mrs. Edmonds and informed her that her "son" Michael was caught stealing in school again. They weren't going to send him home but they wanted her to come to the school in the near future so that they could talk with her about the problem with Michael.

After school while we were walking home, the mood was somber. We all knew that if the school called Mrs. Edmonds and told her what happened she would be furious. We hoped that they wouldn't call.

When we got home all four of us changed our clothes and took to our chores. All of us wondered if Mrs. Edmonds was going to beat Michael. Maybe she didn't know what happened after all. This is what we all hoped. Michael was busy doing his chores, praying that it would all blow over.

That evening just before supper, Mrs. Edmonds summoned us into the kitchen. She had us line up with our backs against the sink. She then told Michael to hold out his hands. When he did, she started screaming at him in a loud voice about how she was sick and tired of the schools calling her up about us and she was going to teach us a lesson. She picked up her leather belt and smacked Michael on the back of his hands real hard. Michael screamed in pain and snatched his hands back in an attempt to protect them from Mrs. Edmonds' brutal beating. She screamed at him, telling him to put his hands back out. Michael was crying and cowering, trying to get away from Mrs. Edmonds' beatings. Mrs. Edmonds snatched him by the arm and pulled his hands out and hit him on them again. Again poor Michael yanked his hands back and turned his back on Mrs. Edmonds, cowering to avoid the onslaught. Mrs. Edmonds pulled Michael by the arm, spinning him around, and started spanking him on his behind; all the while we had to stand there and watch. Arnold flinched each time he heard the strap hit. Tony just stood there with a mean look on his face. I was in tears. We all thought that we would be next after she finished with Michael because she had us lined up at the sink. But we were wrong. And after she stopped beating Michael, she sent him to bed without supper and told us we would get the same thing too if the school called her about us.

"Now go get ready to eat."

Poor Michael ran upstairs holding his hands, crying. I know they had to be burning from the pain. I hated Mrs. Edmonds. Disciplining a child is one thing; brutalizing one is another. And then forcing us to watch as she beat him. . . . We were young; we didn't know the difference. We thought that that was how it was done. Their son Herbert was in the front room watching TV. We could hear him snickering. I knew that it wasn't the TV show that he was watching and snickering at either.

Chapter 5

A Lost Ball in High Grass

Every time we saw a snake, we would tell Tony and then run for our lives. Tony would grab his homemade spear and go after the snake. He wanted to be the hero because he knew that we were afraid of them, especially the big ones like the rattlesnakes. The small grass snakes weren't too bad; they were more afraid of us than we were of them. Tony was fast but not fast enough. I never saw him catch any of the snakes. They always seemed to outrun him. When they did, Tony would come back to the rest of us mad as hell and make up an excuse as to why he couldn't catch the snake. I wanted to tell him that maybe it was his huge ears that slowed him down. When he ran they would flair out in the breeze and slow him down. I dared not tell him that, though.

One day Arnold and I were playing some sort of African jungle game. He was an African native and I was the hunter. Anyway, while I was sitting on the ground planning my next move into the jungle,

Arnold snuck up behind me and stuck a knitting needle in the back of my neck then ran away howling and laughing like a crazy native. Man, was I mad! I ran up to the house and banged on the door. Mrs. Edmonds came to the door with her usual mean attitude and saw me standing on the steps whimpering like a baby. She asked me what I wanted. I told her that Arnold stuck a needle in the back of my neck and it hurt; I guess that made her day. Now she had another reason to punish Arnold. She told me to get back down back and to tell Arnold to come in the house. As I was walking back down into the woods, I thought about what I just did. Now I was really scared, not of the snakes or animals but of Arnold because I told on him, and I knew that he would be mad at me for it.

Anyway, I told him that Mrs. Edmonds said go in the house right now! Arnold started walking towards the house and looked back at me. If looks could kill, I have no doubt that I would be history! Tony and Michael looked at me in disgust. Tony said "Alex, you didn't have to tell on him, you little tattletale." I thought that he was going to punch me in the stomach like Herbie does. I said that I was sorry for telling on Arnold but that needle hurt me.

Mrs. Edmonds made Arnold go up to bed and again he was deprived of his supper; at least she didn't beat him this time. I really felt bad now. He stayed mad at me for a couple of days, and the rest of the guys didn't say much to me either. I remember thinking that the next time when something like that happens I will keep my mouth shut and try to beat up Arnold myself, even though he is bigger than me.

Not long after, Arnold and Tony were playing cowboys and Indians. Arnold was the cowboy—imagine that! Tony let somebody else be the cowboy. Well, Arnold paid for it. When he laid down on the ground playing dead, Tony walked up to him and stuck his homemade spear into the back of Arnold's hand. Arnold jumped up screaming. Tony found an old discarded rag and used it to stop the bleeding, begging Arnold not to tell on him. He looked over at me and gave me that "you better keep your mouth shut this time, or else" look. I guess he remembered the gun incident in Richmond at the Whitmans, and the other day when I told on Arnold. Lucky for Tony, Arnold didn't tell on him. He wasn't a "tattletale" like me. Arnold told Mrs. Edmonds that he hurt his hand while playing with a sharp stick. I guess she believed him because nothing became of it; she gave him a bandage and sent him back outside.

One day I woke up with another one of my headaches. It was Saturday morning, so I didn't have to worry about going to school. Thank God! Because if it was a school day, Mrs. Edmonds would think that I was faking it and make me stay in my room all day. Lately I'd been getting a lot of headaches, and when I did Miz Edmonds would give me an aspirin and tell me to go to my room. That's where I'd spend the entire day: alone in my room. Whenever I had a headache on a Saturday I wouldn't tell Mrs. Edmonds because I knew that she would make me stay in my room all day, and if it was a movie-going day I would have to stay home by myself. So I suffered the pain; most of the time I kept the headaches to myself. I didn't want to have to stay in my room all day. I wanted to be outside with my brothers "down back."

Some of those days "down back" were okay. I guess since we spent so much time in those woods they were our playground, our getaway, our hideout, our world. We played a lot of games "down back," games like tag, hide-and-seek, cowboys and Indians—that was Tony's favorite—marbles that we "purchased" from the South Street Market and whatever else we could think of to pass the time of day in the woods. My favorite was Superman because he was my idol. I used to tuck a rag inside the back of my shirt like a cape and run around the woods like I was the superhero. I used to run into Arnold and Michael and push them on the ground. Both of them would get mad and chase me around the woods. As far as I was concerned they were the bad guys and I was Superman and I had to save the world from them. One day while I was running around like a maniac thinking that I was indestructible, I didn't see the stump in the ground in front of me. Suddenly WHUMP!—I hit the ground face first! *Where the heck did that stump come from?* Arnold and Michael died laughing and Tony just stood there shaking his head as if to say, "You will never learn will you?"

I stood up and dusted myself off, and with all the dignity that I could muster up, I limped off into another part of the woods, mumbling to myself, "The heck with those guys." One thing I realized, I was not Superman; that's for sure. Another time when we were playing hide-and-seek I found a nice hideout behind a large branch lying on the ground. So I dropped down behind it, confident that no one will ever find me. I happened to look to my left and saw something moving. I thought that it was a chipmunk so I paid no attention to it. *Those guys ain't never going to find me,* I thought to myself.

Suddenly that "chipmunk" moved again, only it wasn't a chipmunk—it was a big snake staring at me, flicking his tongue. *Oh, oh, oh, what the heck am I going to do now?* I wondered. I held my breath and tried to figure out what to do. Well, needless to say, panic took over. I jumped up and ran, yelling at the top of my lungs and pointing at the snake.

"Tony! There's a rattlesnake over there in the bushes!" My voice was three octaves higher than normal. Man, I was scared to death. I'm glad I didn't step on him. They would have found me for sure.

Tony came back to where we were laughing and said, "Well, I guess we couldn't find you, but that snake did. Ha, ha, ha!" I didn't think that it was funny at all. Tony liked to make fun of me all the time. I used to get mad at him and want to beat him up, but I knew I couldn't, so I walked away mad. We used to pick on each other all the time. We would call each other names, tell on each other, and fight all the time.

Another time while we were playing hide-and-seek again, I took off into the woods and found a nice spot. This time I made sure that there were no snakes around. I must have gone deep into the woods because I couldn't hear them talking anymore. *Well,* I thought, *they will never find me here.* So I waited and waited. After a while I started feeling uncomfortable about the situation; they should have found me by now, or at least came close to where I was. So I stood up and yelled, "Hey, Arnold, Tony, where are you guys? Betcha can't find me!"

No answer. Now I was getting worried, so I yelled again, this time at the top of my lungs. "Hey you guys, where are you?" Still no answer. Since nobody answered me the second time, I decided to give myself up and come out of my hiding place. The problem was I didn't know where I was. I started walking and couldn't find my way back to our play area. Now I was rally getting scared. I felt like peeing on myself. That's how scared I was. I called out again; still no answer. It was getting to be dusk and the sun was going down. Now panic started to set in. I was getting scared and kept looking out for those guys and snakes too.

I started getting tired of walking, so I sat down to rest. I must have dozed off, because suddenly I heard a loud voice say, "Alex, what the hell are you doing here in these parts of the woods?" I looked up and if I never wanted to see Uncle Charlie, this was one time that I was glad to see him. He said, "Get your butt up and follow me." He smacked me in the back of my flat head and said, "You look like a lost ball in high grass," and walked away chuckling to himself. I followed him like a little puppy out of the woods to the house.

The rest of my brothers were already in the house sitting on the floor, waiting to eat supper. I felt somewhat foolish, but mad at the same time because they didn't come to find me. During supper I kept rolling my eyes at them; they knew that I was mad. They kept avoiding my glares. After supper when we sat back down on the floor, I asked them what happened. Arnold said that they tried to find me but couldn't, and Mrs. Edmonds had knocked on the window for us to come inside. They thought that I had heard the knock too, so they just went inside the house without me. All three of them stuck to the same story. One thing about us: we lied to the Edmondses and we lied to each other. I knew that they were lying but I couldn't prove it, so I let it go.

There were a lot of days when all four of us would become depressed and lonely. We felt unwanted. No one cared about us and nobody wanted to be bothered with us. There were times that we couldn't even stand each other. On those days we all would go to separate spots in the woods and play by ourselves most of the day. Those were the days that we hated each other. We would start fights with each other, and Tony, being the oldest and the biggest, would pick on one of us just to start a fight. Those were the days that we didn't play cowboys and Indians or Superman. It seemed like everybody in the world rejected us, and it took its toll on us. We felt that we were not worth anything to anybody, not even to each other. Those days I would daydream about my mother, wondering how she looked and where she was.

I remember when school was letting out for the summer, all of the other the kids talked about going on vacation with their parents and going places like on fishing trips with their fathers or maybe camping with the whole family. When school opened back up in the fall the kids would talk about where they gone for their vacation, places such as Disney World, New York City, the beaches. All kinds of activities. I used to sit and listen to them, feeling empty; my summer vacation consisted of going to summer camp for two weeks. The rest of the summer was spent "down back."

Chapter 6

The "Bully"

One day while we were down back playing, minding our own business, Herbie came down to where we were. I said, "Here comes Herbie. I bet he wants to bother us and beat on us or something. He must be bored." But this time I was wrong. I could tell that there was something wrong with him because he had a real mean look on his face. He stood there for a minute with his hands on his hips, looking at all four of us.

Tony asked him, "What's was the matter?"

Herbie said, "Which one of you little sons of bitches stole my watch? Whoever has it better give it back to me right now!" I looked over at Michael because I knew that he had a bad habit of stealing, especially watches. There was something about watches that Michael liked. All four of us looked at each other puzzled. We had no idea what he was talking about. When no one answered him, he grabbed Tony by the arm and shouted at him, saying, "I want my goddamn watch now, dammit!"

Tony attempted to pull away from Herbie but he couldn't because Herbie was bigger and held on real tight. He finally let go of Tony's arm. He looked at me, and said, "Alex, which one of you little shitheads stole my watch?" I guess he thought that because I told on Arnold before, I was a tattletale, and that I would tell on the one that took his watch.

I said, "Herbie, I don't know who took your watch."

He said, "Stop lying, you know who's got my watch." He then punched me in the stomach real hard, causing me to double over in pain. I tried not to cry but my stomach was hurting, and the tears started coming to my eyes.

He walked over to Arnold and said "I bet you are the one that took my watch; you look like a god damn thief anyway!" With that he punched Arnold in the stomach. Arnold fell to his knees, groaning in pain. Herbie was just about to go after Michael, when out of nowhere came Tony holding a large tree branch like a baseball bat. He had a crazy look in his eyes. He shouted at Herbie, telling him to go away and leave us the f##k alone. I thought that Herbie was going to try to take the limb from Tony but he didn't. Tony told him that none of us had his watch and we didn't know what he was talking about. Herbie stood there for a minute trying to decide what to do next. Tony still held on to the tree branch firmly and he looked like he was ready to use it if he had to. Herbie finally gave up and turned and walked away, mumbling to himself about how he was going to get his watch back one way or another.

That's the first time I ever heard Tony swear. We were all stunned because we had never heard Tony swear before. He seemed like he had become a different person. I asked Michael if he had taken Herbie's watch; he said he didn't and that I shouldn't be accusing him.

I said, "I wasn't accusing you, I just wanted to know."

Michael said, "Even if I did you probably would have told on me anyway because you're a tattletale."

When he called me a tattletale, I got mad and called him a thief. I said, "You probably did steal Herbie's watch."

Suddenly Michael pushed me and we both fell to the ground. We started fighting with each other. We punched and scratched and kicked. I even tried to poke his eyes out. He kept hitting me on my head and back. We both rolled around on the ground, trying to kill each other. Arnold and finally jumped in and pulled us apart. The fight was brought on by frustration, we all knew that, but we couldn't help it. Fighting with each other relieved the frustration.

We later found out what had happened. One morning when Herbie was washing his hands, he laid his watch on the sink and it fell in a trashcan that was on the floor beside the sink. He must have forgotten about it, and then noticed it missing later. That's when he came down back and accused us of taking it. We were all mad as hell at him for that, and Tony still wanted to beat him with that tree branch! That was the first time we ever saw Tony stand up to any of the Edmondses. Man, he had nerve! We all thought that Herbie would tell his mother, Mrs. Edmonds, about what had happened but he didn't. Not right away, that is. I think Tony was at the point where he didn't care what happened to him anymore. He felt that it was his place to protect us, his little brothers.

When one of us got a beating, we cried for him. We felt the pain ourselves. We used to hear Mrs. Edmonds yelling at the top of her lungs at whoever she was beating, and we could hear the board as it was hitting him. The crying and the screaming and the constant Whack! Whack! Whack! traumatized the rest of us. What an evil woman she was.

Mrs. Edmonds didn't allow us to play with the other kids in the neighborhood. I guess she thought that we would tell them how she was treating us. These were kids our own age, living on our street, and we couldn't associate with them. Some of the kids would come over to our house to make friends with us and play with us "down back," but Mrs. Edmonds would always find a reason to send them away, telling them that we had chores to take care of or that we were on punishment, which was probably true. She always had that big flat board handy to beat us with if we "misbehaved." I guess she didn't want any of the other kids to witness the brutal beatings she gave us with it.

Chapter 7

Uncle Charlie's Secrets

Uncle Charlie Edmonds still kept taking Arnold away from us to go to work in the charcoal kiln. At least this is what we were led to believe.

In later years, Arnold would come to Springfield to visit me from Colorado from time to time. Each time he would tell me that he had something to tell me, but he never did. One day when he was here visiting, he broke down and told me what was on his mind. We were sitting around chatting about different things and I could sense that there was something on his mind. I asked him was everything all right with him in Colorado?

He said, "I have no problems in Colorado; my problem is here. Remember when I told you that I had something to tell you?"

I said, "I remember."

He said, "I don't want to talk about it here. Can we go some place in private so we can talk?"

I said, "Sure, let's go get a pizza." So we went to a nearby pizza parlor and that's when he revealed what was on his mind.

He said, "You guys never knew what was going on in that charcoal place in Pittsfield with Uncle Charlie." He said that Uncle Charlie made him do filthy things to him. He said that he dreaded the days that Uncle Charlie would come down back and take him to the kiln. He knew what was going to happen once they got there. He said that Uncle Charlie would drive him up to the kiln in his green 1954 Chrysler.

Once they arrived, Uncle Charlie would take him into his small office. There he would spread an old potato sack on the floor and force Arnold to lie down on it. Uncle Charlie would then drop his pants down around his ankles and squat over Arnold's face and masturbate, and at the same time defecate on Arnold's face. He tried to force Arnold to open his mouth and eat the defecation but the smell would make Arnold throw up.

Uncle Charlie kept making moaning and grunting noises and forcing his penis in Arnold's mouth, gagging him. Arnold would try to get up off of the floor, but Uncle Charlie used his weight and kept pushing him back down with his body. Arnold would cry and beg Uncle Charlie to stop and told him that he wanted to go back home. But Uncle Charlie was obsessed and he would not let Arnold up. He had a large mirror leaning up against a wall. He used this mirror to watch himself as he masturbated. He would grind his testicles in Arnold's face and tell Arnold to "lick my balls," and then ejaculate in Arnold's mouth, forcing Arnold to swallow it.

Arnold said that this went on for about an hour each time. And after Uncle Charlie Edmonds got through with him he would wash him up and threaten him by telling him that he better not ever tell anyone about this or else he would be sorry. He then drove Arnold back home and sent him back down back as if nothing happened.

Arnold went on to say that oftentimes when we were all "down back," Uncle Charlie would bring him into the house and force him to have oral sex in the kitchen, and he would give Arnold a glass of milk before forcing him to perform oral sex. This he repeated a couple of times; milk first, oral sex after. To this day I don't know what the milk thing was and neither does Arnold. Arnold said this started when he was seven years old and continued until he was ten. All the while we thought that he was helping Uncle Charlie Edmonds in the charcoal kiln.

Good old "Uncle Charlie" our "friend."

He said that sometimes when we all were at the kiln packing charcoal, Uncle Charlie would take him away from the rest of us into his office and sexually abuse him. None of the rest of us had any idea of what was going on. Uncle Charlie" never took any of the rest of us to the kiln for sex.

I asked him why didn't he tell us or at least tell Tony. He said that he thought that Tony would make fun of him and that he was ashamed of himself. And Uncle Charlie told him that he better not ever tell anybody. I said, "Arnold, you were only seven years old. Who would blame you?"

He said that at the time and having the mind of a seven-year-old, he didn't know how to handle it and he felt that we would laugh at him. I asked him why it took him so long to tell me. He said that he felt that I would turn my back on him and think the worst of him. He said that for a long time he felt as though it was his fault that those things happened to him. He couldn't understand why Uncle Charlie did those things to him and not the rest of us. I wondered myself! He said that many times he wanted to run away with Tony but was too afraid.

While we were talking that day, Arnold reached inside his waistband and pulled out a fully loaded .38 snub-nose revolver and said, "I am going to go to Pittsfield and kill that son of a bitch for what he did to me! So he won't be able to do it to any more kids!" Arnold said that he thought Mrs. Edmonds knew what Uncle Charlie was doing to him, and that was why she treated him like she did. She was taking her frustrations out on Arnold.

I could see the look in his eyes and I knew that he was not joking. He meant it. He said his plans were to go to Pittsfield, shoot both Mrs. Edmonds and Uncle Charlie, and then "take off" back to Colorado, where nobody would ever find him.

Arnold said that another reason it took him so long to tell me was because he didn't want me to know that he was planning on killing the Edmondses. Right then and there I knew that I had to convince him that he was making a big mistake and that eventually he would get caught and end up spending the rest of his life in prison. I told him that Uncle Charlie wasn't worth him spending the rest of his life in jail. I said that the miserable bastard will get what's coming to him in time. I finally convinced him, because he handed me the gun and just sat there staring into space as if he was in a trance.

I could tell that this was something he had planned for a long time, and he was bent on carrying out his plans. I'm just glad that he told me about his plans instead of carrying them out. One cannot imagine the frustrations and torment and anger one carries inside. But then on the other hand, how do you tell someone that has been humiliated and abused that—*it's not worth it?*

A few years later, Arnold did return to Pittsfield and confronted Uncle Charlie, asking him why he did those things to him. Uncle Charlie's answer was because it happened to him when he was a child! Arnold said, "I guess he meant that because it happened to him, it was all right to abuse other children." That was the wrong answer. God only knows how many other children he may have abused. Arnold said that during his conversation with Uncle Charlie, Mrs. Edmonds was on the telephone telling her granddaughter Patsy that Arnold was there for revenge! And she was afraid of him. Arnold said he was there just to find out why Uncle Charlie did what he did to him. Something that he will never forget!

Chapter 8

"Now I Lay Me Down to Sleep"

Just about every night while we were in bed for the night, Edith or Mrs. Edmonds would sneak up the stairs to see if we were talking in the bed. Talking in bed at the Edmonds house was a cardinal sin. And whenever we got caught we would get slapped in the mouth. Most of the time, it would be me. I had a habit of telling my brothers stories at bedtime. It was something I liked doing, making up stories and telling them. I never told them the end of the story the same night, probably because most of the time I didn't know how I was going to end it anyway. I guess I was being rather bold doing that, but I took my chances. I would start my story in a whisper, listening for the stairs to creak. The Edmondses' house was old, and the staircase was very squeaky. Every time one of them tried to sneak up those stairs we could hear them, especially Edith. She was a big person; she was like an elephant trying to tiptoe on eggshells without breaking them. As soon as she started, we could hear the methodical *squeak, squeak, squeak,* then we would get real quiet hoping that whoever it was would go back downstairs and leave us alone. At times they would trick us. We would think that they had gone back downstairs when in fact they would be still standing on the stairs waiting to catch us talking again. Then, of course, when they heard us they would come into the room and ask who it was that was talking. I would get told on and get a slap in the mouth and told to shut up and go to sleep! I would be angry with the person who told on me and promise myself that I would never tell him a story again!

Until I cooled off that is.

We loved it when the Edmondses left us alone to go into town to shop. There was a big pine tree in the back of the house and every time the Edmondses left, Arnold would climb the tree and be our lookout. You could see halfway down the road from the top of the tree. One time while Arnold was scampering up the tree he fell out of it and landed on his butt. We all laughed but that didn't stop him—up the tree he went again, making sure that the Edmondses didn't double back. When the coast was clear we would dash into the house and help ourselves to whatever goodies we could find such as cake or cookies, sweets that we could never enjoy with the rest of the family. Each time we went into the house, Michael would drift off into another room. We knew that he was looking for something to steal besides food. He would go into the bedrooms and living room looking for "stuff." When we got ready to leave we could never find Michael. We always had to call out to him and tell him that we were leaving. Then he would emerge from another room, probably with something in his pockets.

Tony said, "Come on, let's get out of here before they get back." We knew that Arnold was getting tired of sitting in that tree.

We then retreated back into the woods, and Arnold would come out of the tree and get his share of the booty. On occasions the Edmondses would take off on vacations and leave us alone with Edith and Herbie. Both of them were brutal. Edith used to work in a hospital; I think she was a nurse. In my opinion, she was cold-hearted and cruel; it was hard to believe she was a nurse. She may have been a cleaning person. I never really knew what she did, but she always wore a uniform. We would ask Edith for some more food to eat, and she would say, "If I thought you deserved some more food I would give it to you, so don't ask me no more! Sit your behind down on the floor and shut up!" So all four of us would leave the table with half-empty stomachs as usual, and big Edith picked one of us to wash the dishes.

Herbie wasn't too bad. When the Edmondses left I guess he still remembered the incident with Tony. We noticed that ever since that watch incident, he kept his distance from us. After dinner Edith and Patsy would go into the living room and watch TV. Herbie would be listening to his doo-wop, and we would be sitting on the floor in the vestibule, waiting to get sent to bed.

Each year as we got older and our birthdays came, we never had the luxury of having anybody sing "Happy Birthday" to us, or give us birthday presents. Never did anyone ever say, "Happy birthday, Alex," or, "Happy birthday, Tony," or Michael or Arnold. We used to make our own presents in the woods out of tree branches and give it to whose ever birthday it was. Then we would get in a circle and Tony would lead us in song, singing "Happy Birthday." Sometimes when we started singing real loud, Mrs. Edmonds would open the kitchen window and yell at us to be quiet. I think her conscience bothered her, if she had one!

We were all getting older; Tony was getting real tall and lanky. He would swagger when he walked, trying his best to walk like a cowboy. Arnold, my twin, was bigger than me. Michael was six years old and he had a rather large head. We used to call him "big head," which made him very upset, and off to the other part of the woods he would go. He was very quiet. Michael kept pretty much to himself most of the time. He didn't talk much at all. It was difficult at times trying to get Michael to talk and play with the rest of us. Michael was getting a little bigger now. He looked like he was half white. There were times when he wouldn't play cowboys with the rest of us; most of the time he would go somewhere by himself and play with his little red truck. He had a real bad temper.

Chapter 9

"Cowboys and Indians"

One Friday evening while we were busy doing our chores, Tony came running from out of the house. We thought that something had happened. We knew that he had gone inside to go to the bathroom, something he always did to try to get out of doing his share of the chores. We knew that he was excited about something, so we gathered around him and asked him what was going on. He said that Mrs. Edmonds told him that if we behaved maybe she would let us go to the movies tomorrow! That was good news. We couldn't wait for tomorrow to come. We were all excited about going. Tony said he heard that there was a good cowboy movie playing. I wanted to see *Batman and Robin.*

The next day we got up, did our chores, and scurried down back, waiting for Mrs. Edmonds to knock on the window so we could get going to the movies. When the knock came we all filed out of the woods and waited for Mrs. Edmonds to come outside. She came out and gave Tony the money for the movies, telling us that we'd better behave and get home right after the movies. We all said, "Yes, Miz Edmonds," and we started on our way, laughing and joking around with each other. Suddenly shouted out to Arnold, asking him where he thought he was going. She was standing there with her hands on her hips looking mean as usual. Arnold turned around and looked at her. Puzzled, he said, "To the movies with them," pointing at us.

"Oh no you don't! When you learn to behave yourself and come home from school on time I'll let you go. Now get your behind down back right now!"

Arnold stood there for a moment in disbelief. He thought that he had already been punished for that. He had no idea what she was talking about. He said, "Mrs. Edmonds, I didn't do nothin' bad."

She shouted at him, "Don't get smart with me." And with that she slapped him across the face and told him to "get out of her sight." Arnold put his hands to his face and ran back down back in tears. We watched him as he sat on the water heater with his head down. We knew that he was crying, but what could we do?

Mrs. Edmonds was cold-hearted and cruel. She enjoyed tormenting us, especially Arnold. She knew that going to the movies was something that we all looked forward to. And for her to keep Arnold from going was cruel and heartless. Arnold had done nothing wrong at all. As the rest of us started walking to the movies in silence, Uncle Charlie came out of the house and called Arnold up from the woods. He was still crying. Uncle Charlie told Mrs. Edmonds that since Arnold couldn't go to the movies he was taking him to the kiln to help him pack charcoal. We felt bad for Arnold. Tony was saying something about taking Arnold with him the next time he ran away, and maybe we all should run away with him.

"Where would we go?" I asked him.

"I don't know," he answered, "just away from here."

Eventually we arrived at the movies, but it just wasn't the same without Arnold. At least he was with Uncle Charlie helping out at the kiln.

Some of the movies that we used to watch featured old cowboy favorites such as Roy Rogers and Dale Evans, Gene Autry, and Hop-Along Cassidy. I loved watching all of the characters in the cartoons that used to come on before the main feature such as Bugs Bunny, Donald Duck, Mickey Mouse, and Pluto. Tony was in love with the cowboy movies.

After we left the movies and returned "down back," Arnold was already down back playing. We told him about the movies, and Tony would start his cowboy thing, thinking that he was Billy the Kid. Then the arguments would start. He wanted us to be the bad guys again. We got tired of being the bad guys all of the time. Sometimes we wanted to be the good guys, but Tony always wanted to be the hero. I wanted to be the hero for a change. I wanted to be a Texas Ranger. Yeah! A Texas Ranger: that's what I wanted to be, just like in the movies. But Tony had to have his way, and if he didn't he would chase us around the woods with his homemade spear or stalk off into another part of the woods singing a cowboy song like, *"Oh give me a home where da buffalo roam."* We could hear him playing cowboy by himself, shooting his toy guns that we got for Christmas and making shooting noises with his mouth—*Bang! Bang!*—and talking to imaginary bad guys, trying real hard to talk with that Western drawl. The only thing he was missing was the bowlegs and cowboys boots. We couldn't tell him anything—he was Roy Rogers, King of the Cowboys.

In school we used to make coonskin caps out of paper, then when we got home we would play Davy Crockett and build a little Alamo with tree branches and limbs. There was no question as to who Davy Crockett was and who the bad guys were.

Chapter 10
Clapp Park

In the center of Pittsfield there was a small park called Clapp Park. Every now and then Mrs. Edmonds would let us go there. On our way to the park we would take a shortcut through a parking lot.

Clapp Park

One day while we were cutting through on our way to the park, Tony saw a Table Talk Pie truck with the back door open. It was parked in the lot with no one around. So, being "Mr. Bold One," Tony looked around to see if anyone was coming then he jumped into the back of the truck. He found a whole stack of pies in boxes in the rear of the truck. Quickly he grabbed a handful and passed them out to us and jumped down. We then took off to the park with our pies.

It must have been a funny sight to see four colored boys sitting up on top of a hill, eating whole pies. What a mess we made! Our hands and faces were covered with blueberries, apples, and peaches from the pie fillings. You can believe that we cleaned up before we went back home. We ate so many of those pies we made ourselves sick. Our stomachs were bloated but we were happy. Each time that we were allowed to go to the park we looked for a pie truck but never saw anymore after that day.

Clapp Park was where the neighborhood kids hung around and played baseball. Tony had a way with the kids in the park, especially the bad kids. They even let him play ball with them. One day while we were at the park and Tony was playing baseball with some of the kids, I decided that I wanted to play too. So I ran, or should I say, I started to run across the field to see if I could play baseball too. I guess my timing was a little off. Tony was at bat, and just as I dashed across the field he hit the ball. The next thing I knew I was on the ground with a busted lip and a black eye. Tony had hit that ball just right. It hit me dead in the mouth, knocking me to the ground.

You would think that he would stop to see if I was all right. No way. Tony dashed around the diamond, hoping to make a home run. I was sitting on the ground, crying like a baby with a busted lip and a swollen jaw. Tony was in his own world, scoring a home run. The rest of my brothers ran over to me and helped me up. I was mad at Tony for that and wanted to beat him up. I promised myself that one day when I grew up I would beat Tony up for not helping me after he hit me with the baseball.

There were a lot of bad kids hanging around in Clapp Park. I remember the first time we went to the park we saw some older kids playing baseball and every time one of them missed the ball another one would call him a name like "asshole." This was the first time I had ever heard those words that they were saying to each other. They were telling each other to kiss their asses and "f##k you." They were calling each other names like "sons o' bitches" and "motherf##kers." We thought it was funny when one of the kids called another a name and told him to "kiss his ass." They would start fighting with each other. The only time I ever heard a swear word was when Tony swore at Herbie that day in the woods when he accused us of taking his watch.

As the day went on we started repeating the swears. We started calling each other those new names. We thought that it was funny swearing at each other. When a white kid ran by us and called us "niggers," we didn't think that was funny at all. Tony wanted to fight. We knew that that was a bad idea because we were the only colored kids in the park! On the way home we continued to call each other those names. I called Tony an "asshole." Arnold called me a "shithead,"

Tony called me a "son of a bitch," Michael called Arnold an "asshole." I told all of them to "kiss my ass" as loud as I could. Four little colored kids running down South Street swearing and laughing at each other at the top of our lungs; I'm sure the local residents thought that we were crazy. We were having a ball. When we got back down back we kept it up, and Tony came up with a new swear that none of us knew. He called me a "cocksu##er"—he said that he learned that one in school but was afraid to say it in front of us because he thought that I might tell the Edmondses that he was saying a bad word.

One day soon after we learned our new vocabulary, Mrs. Edmonds was scolding Tony about something he had done. While she was screaming at him, I looked at his face and I could have sworn that he was repeating under his breath those new words that he had learned at the park. He had that look on his face. I prayed that he didn't slip up and say, "F##k you!" to her. I held my breath and prayed real hard. She kept yelling at Tony. It seemed like it would go on forever. Whatever it was that Tony had or hadn't done really made her mad; she would not let up. I knew that any minute he would let loose with the new vocabulary we had learned. I guess she finally ran out of steam and stopped screaming. She pointed towards us and said, "Now get your behind down back with the rest of them."

Tony turned around and swaggered down back to where we were. We all gathered around him, and as soon as we were sitting in our little powwow circle on the hot water heater, all of the swear words that we had learned in Clapp Park came out of Tony's mouth in rapid succession, along with words that I had never heard at the park! I guess if Mrs. Edmonds ever heard us repeating the swear words that we learned at the park, our park days would be over for good! More than once we all at some point wanted to practice our new vocabulary on Mrs. Edmonds and tell her how we felt.

Chapter 11

School Days

The first-grade school that we went to was a little one-room school called Moorewood School, located on South Mountain Road in Pittsfield. One day while at school, the teacher asked Michael to go get something for her. I guess Michael took too long to get it, so she shouted at him to "hurry up and shake a leg." At that point Michael must have misunderstood what she meant and he stopped walking and started shaking his leg. I thought I would die laughing; the whole class thought it was funny and started laughing. The teacher did not think that it was funny at all, and she showed it by whacking Michael on the behind with a ruler and telling him that he was not a comedian. Michael was a quiet kid, very grumpy. We had heard that his parents were mixed: his father was "colored" and his mother was "white." He did look a little mixed up; he was real light skinned with curly black hair. I think Tony was half white too, but his hair was "nappy"; both of them probably had parents that resented them, causing them to be placed in the D.C.G.

Moorewood School—then

(*Courtesy of Pittsfield Library*)

Moorewood School—now

Plunkett School

(Courtesy of Pittsfield Library)

Redfield School

(Courtesy of Pittsfield Library)

In school I sat next to a girl named Susan. She was a real cute girl. Every day at lunchtime she would share her lunch with me. She used to have ham and cheese sandwiches neatly wrapped in plastic sandwich wraps, along with fruit and pastries. She along with the other kids had milk with their lunch. We didn't. Instead, the teacher would give us a cup of water. Mrs. Edmonds was supposed to pay for our milk with the milk money the state allotted her. I guess she felt that we didn't deserve the three-cent milk. Every now and then an anonymous person paid for our milk. I think Susan brought all that food to school because she knew that I would want some and felt sorry for me, or maybe she liked me; all I know is that I was in *love* with her and I wanted to take her home with me "down back" and live happily ever after.

All of the other kids in school had cute little lunch boxes with their favorite cartoon characters on them. We had to carry our lunch to school in used-up old wrinkled paper bags still greasy from the day before. It was a school policy that when you arrived at school in the morning, you gave your lunch to the teacher. Then at lunchtime she would call each child to the front of the class to pick up his or her lunch. Every time the teacher called one of us three to get our lunch, the rest of the kids would start giggling and making fun of us with our wrinkled bags. We dared not throw the bags away because Miz Edmonds made it very clear that she wanted to use the bags for as long as they would last. Most of the time our sandwiches consisted of sandwich spread with pickles. Arnold used to throw his away and eat whatever we took from the stores. The sandwiches tasted awful. Sometimes Mrs. Edmonds would change up and give us peanut butter and jelly sandwiches. The sandwich spread would leak out of the tinfoil that she wrapped our sandwiches in, and after a couple of days the bags would be nice and greasy but Mrs. Edmonds continued to use them for as long as she could.

Another school that I went to was called Redfield School, located in the center of Pittsfield. I don't remember seeing any other colored kids in Redfield School. I remember one day when school was being dismissed, and as I started to leave the classroom, my teacher Mrs. Pennington called me to her desk. She said, "Alexander, I don't want to offend you but I have a question to ask you."

I said, "Yes, Mrs. Pennington?"

Then she asked me, "How would someone of your race prefer to be called when someone addresses you, 'colored' or 'Negro'?"

I was totally confused and didn't know how to answer her, so I just shrugged my shoulders and said, "I don't know, Mrs. Pennington. Negro I guess."

Most of the kids in school were okay. We all got along together, but there was one incident that I remember. One day while I was on my way to class in Redfield School, this white kid name John was standing in the hallway trying to take off his watch. He finally got it off, and when he did it fell on the floor. I instinctively went to pick it up for him. Why did I do that? He screamed at me at the top of his lungs to take my "black nigger hands" off of his watch. That made me mad and I wanted to fight. I pushed him, but before we could get started Mrs. Pennington, the same teacher who asked me about being "colored" or "Negro," intervened. She asked us what happened. I told her that

John called me a nigger. She asked John if he did and, of course, he lied and said, "No, Mrs. Pennington." She believed him and told me to stop trying to start trouble, and told us both to get in the classroom. I was really mad now. I told John that I was going to beat him up after school. At the end of the day I looked for John outside to finish our discussion about race, but he was nowhere to be found.

There was another school called Plunkett School that we went to. I remember a girl named Sharon. She used to wear her blonde hair in pigtails. She had big blue eyes behind thick, horn-rimmed glasses. I thought that she was pretty, maybe a little on the blind side, but smart. I liked her. I think her father was a policeman.

All during our stay in Pittsfield, we went to quite a few different schools. Tony went to Pittsfield High, Arnold went to Plunkett, and Michael and I went to Redfield School. I don't know why we went to all those different schools. I didn't like any of them. I liked looking at the girls in school, Susan and Sharon; other than that I hated school with a passion. All of the schools were a long way from our house and we had a certain time by which we had to get home after school or suffer the consequences. Every now and then, out of the goodness of her heart, Mrs. Edmonds would give us bus tickets and we would catch the yellow school bus. Tony used to sell his tickets and walk to school. I often wondered if he even went to school.

God forbid if we brought home a bad report card. If we did we would be put on punishment and get a beating. Every time one of us got a bad report card we would "fix" it so that no one would get a beating. "Fixing" a report card meant changing the failing marks on it to passing marks such as F to B or an E to a B. It took a little bit of artwork but it worked most of the time.

I remember one particular day that I didn't get a chance to doctor up my report card. It was not a good one. I hated the thought of going home. I knew that my behind was going to get beat. As I walked home from school with the bad report card, I knew what was going to happen when I got there. When Mrs. Edmonds saw my report card, I can't begin to describe the vicious whipping I got. It seemed like Mrs. Edmonds went into a frenzy. She told me to take off my pants and told me to bend over the chair that she always used when she's whipped us. She took the flat wooden paddle that she used and started banging away on me. I tried to break free but she held onto my arm real tight and kept hitting me as hard as she could—*whack! whack! whack!* She hit me as hard as she could, screaming at me that "this is what you get for having a bad report card." She repeatedly called me a "stupid, nappy-headed, good-for-nothing little nigger." She kept swinging the board, and each time it hit me I felt a burning pain. It seemed like she would never stop. My rear end was burning from the hardwood board but she kept it up.

Finally she stopped and sent me down back crying my heart out. I knew it affected my brothers because they were real quiet and solemn when I joined them in the woods. I could see the compassionate looks on their faces. They all knew how I felt because it happened to them more than once and it would happen to all of us again and again. Tony came up to me and put his arm around me and sat me down in our little circle. We all agreed on how much we hated the Edmondses and wished that we could leave there forever.

These were the times that we really wanted to be with our real mothers and fathers. Many nights we would lie in bed wondering where our real parents were. Every time one of us would get a whipping, Tony would come and embrace the unfortunate victim and show his compassion. He would always have us all sit down in our little circle on the hot water heater and say things to comfort us. I guess he figured since he was the oldest it was his place to comfort us in our time of need. When he got his share of beatings, Tony would shy away from the rest of us and go off into another part of the woods by himself, probably planning when he would run away again. Eventually he would come back and start playing with us. We would play cowboys and Indians, and since Tony was the one that got the beating, the rest of us volunteered to be Indians that day. Tony was in his glory then. I guess he thought that he had to get his butt whipped in order for us to volunteer to be the bad guys.

One day while Arnold and I were walking home from school a small gray car pulled over to the curb with a strange-looking man in it. He looked at us and signaled for us to come over to his car. He was fat and had a weird look on his face. He was slightly bald and was wearing thin eyeglasses. He looked like some sort of "weirdo." When we got near the car he said, "Hi, fellas! I couldn't help but notice that you guys look like you could use something to eat. Are you hungry" I guess because of our appearance we looked like we were starving. We were thin and shabby looking. Everybody that saw us figured that we were starving—we were!

We both nodded our heads and said, "Well, sort of."

He said, "Come get in the car and I take you to get something to eat."

As Arnold started to get into the car, I grabbed him by the arm and said, "Arnold, wait. Remember what our schoolteacher told us? Our teacher told us never to talk to strangers, or accept a ride from someone that we didn't know." And this guy was really strange. So we backed up from the car and turned and walked away at a real fast pace. The man sat there a little longer then drove off. As he was driving away I noticed a different look on his face. It wasn't the kind and caring face he had a minute ago. Now he looked mean and scary. As both of us ran down the street Arnold asked me why we didn't go with the man. I said that he looked strange and I didn't trust him, and that he looked like the kind of man the teachers in school always warned us kids about. When we got to school we told the teacher about what happened and she asked us what he looked like. She said that she was going to report it to the principal, and maybe she would call the police.

Another day while the four of us were on our way to school, we saw a dead body lying in a stream under the bridge that we crossed every morning on our way to school. It looked like a young boy about our age. There was something hanging out of his mouth. It looked like his tongue. Whatever it was, it was all wrinkled up from the water. There were a lot of people there, with some detectives and an ambulance. There was a small, gray car parked across the street with a strange-looking man in it. He looked like the same man that tried to pick up Arnold and me. I wondered if that man had something to do with the boy in the stream.

Chapter 12

Miss Hackleberry

I never considered us as bad kids, but we got into our share of trouble in Pittsfield. There was a little store on South Street called the South Street Market, and every day while on the way to school we did a little "shopping." There were all sorts of candy and baseball cards with bubble gum inside. There used to be an old lady that worked there named Miss Hackleberry. She whore thick, horn-rimmed glasses down on the end of her nose. They looked like Coca-Cola bottles, and she wore her hair in a huge bun tied in the back of her head. She kind of reminded me of the lady standing with her husband holding the pitchfork on the front of the Kellogg's Corn Flakes cereal box. Her regular customers called her "Abby," short for Abigail.

Miss Hackleberry dreaded every time we entered the store. As soon as we entered the store she would focus her little beady eyes right on us! She knew what we were up to. We all wore oversized coats with the inside pockets torn out so anything that we put in our pockets would fall into the seam of the coat. We used to fill our pockets up. The way we did it was when we entered the store, Arnold would ask in a loud voice, "Where is the lady?" meaning Miss Hackleberry, so as to draw her attention away from the rest of us. We knew that she was watching us. Arnold would ask her where a certain item was and all the while the rest of us were loading up our pockets. After we loaded up we left the store and headed for school, laughing at old Miss Abby. She was highly upset with us again because she didn't catch us.

I remember another day when we "hit" the store. Our pockets were full of candy and gum, and as we ran down the street laughing, we ran smack-dab into a big, fat policeman. He said, "All right, hold it right there. I'm Officer Haskell and I know what you boys are up to. I'm tired of that lady in the store telling me about you boys stealing."

He asked us what we had in our pockets. We told him some candy that we bought. He didn't believe us. I think he already knew that we stole it. He made us go back to the store and empty our pockets out on the counter in front of Abigail Hackleberry. Old Miss Hackleberry was in her glory now. She gave us a look as if to say, "I'm glad you guys got caught, and I hope that you all go to jail for the rest of your lives." That's the look she gave us. But she didn't say anything to us in front of the fat policeman.

After we finished unloading our pockets, the policeman took us outside and gave us a lecture about how bad stealing was and where we could end up if we kept it up. As he was talking to us, I glanced back at the store and saw old Miss Hackleberry looking out the window at us. She had a smug look on her wrinkled face; she loved every minute of it.

After the policeman finished his lecture, he went inside and spoke with old Abby and then came outside, and to our surprise he reached inside his pockets and gave us each a quarter and said, "Now go and buy yourself some candy and get on to school." He was fat and old but real nice. I think something old Abigail said to him made him mad, so he gave us money to buy candy right in front of Miss Abigail. He then walked away, whistling. We filed back into the store and old Abby started huffing and puffing. I guess she thought that we were going to say something to her about the policeman but we didn't say a word. We picked our candy off of the shelves and started for the counter.

Miss Hackleberry said, "You better be paying for that candy or I will tell the policeman on you again!" When she threatened to tell on us again, one of those new swear words that I learned at Clapp Park came into my mind, something like "f##k you!" But luckily for Abby those words stayed in my mind and didn't come out of my mouth. We paid for our candy with the money that officer Haskell gave us, and as we left the store we all stuck our tongues out at old Abigail Huckleberry. I think Tony showed her one of his fingers. She looked down at us over her Coca-Cola bottles and mumbled something incoherently under her breath, probably calling us "little colored assholes." I wonder if she ever hung out at Clapp Park!

Off to school we went.

There was another little market called Boyd's Market on South Street. It was a little store with lots of candy, gum, and pastries. One of my favorite candies was the little fake wax soda bottles filled with juice. I drank the juice out then chewed the wax like gum. Another favorite was the *good&plentys* pink and white candy capsules that came in a box. Every now and then we would skip over going to the South Street Market and "shop" at Boyd's Market. One day while I was in school munching on some *Mike&Ikes* candy that I "purchased" from Boyd's Market, the teacher told me to report to the principal's office right now. *Uh-oh!* I thought. *What did I do now?*

When I got to the office I saw a big white man wearing a large trench coat and a wide-brimmed hat that was pulled halfway down over his face. I couldn't see his eyes but he had a real mean look on his face. He looked like one of the detectives we saw at the stream with the dead kid. He looked at me and said in a mean voice, "I'm Detective Mullins." He then asked me what my name was. I think he already knew it but was trying to scare me. Well, if he was he was doing a good job of it. He asked me what did I have in my pockets, but before I could answer he said in a stern voice, "Empty your pockets right now!"

I knew that I was in for it now. My pockets were full of stolen bubble gum and candy from Boyd's Market. I was petrified. My mouth was dry and I was trembling. The detective pointed at the candy and gum and asked me, "Where did you get all that stuff from?" He already knew but he wanted to hear it from me where it came from. I tried to answer him but started stuttering. The detective said, "SHUT UP! And listen to me very carefully."

He then read me the riot act and told me what he would do to me if he ever caught me stealing candy again. He was not nice like the fat policeman. After school when all four of us got together, we talked about what happened in school that day and found out that the same detective had talked to Michael and Arnold and Tony in their schools too. We all were nervous about what happened and agreed to stay away from all of the stores in Pittsfield, Massachusetts, for the rest of our lives. (Or a couple of days!)

There was a little game that we used to play on the way to school, and that was called "scoop the dimes and dash." Back in the fifties most of the "mom-and-pop" stores in downtown Pittsfield sold newspapers in front of their stores on the sidewalk. Newspaper vendors would drop a pile of papers in front of the stores and pedestrians would drop a dime on the pile and take a paper. Eventually the pile of dimes grew. There were even a few nickels and some quarters! We knew about how long it would take for the pile of dimes to grow, so we waited and waited and finally, when we thought the pile was big enough for all four of us to split up, we struck like lightning! We were sure to watch out for the fat policeman and that mean detective man. At least now we had money to buy candy and not steal it. After all, stealing was bad; the fat policeman had told us.

Chapter 13

Here Comes the State Man

It was a standard policy for the Department of Child Guardianship (D.C.G.) to send a social worker (state man) to foster homes to check on the well-being of the foster children in those homes. Prior to each visit, the state man would call and notify Mrs. Edmonds that he was coming. This gave her a chance to prepare us for the visit. She would have us go up to our room and change into our "good" clothes. I guess she didn't want the state man to see us looking ragged. She was supposed to buy us new clothes from time to time but she never did. Instead, she would give us clothes that were handed down from other members of the family. All of our clothes were ragged, our shirts had holes in the sleeves, and our sneakers had holes in the front of them. They looked like they had tongues. When we walked they would open up in the front and you could see our toes flapping.

Before the state man came, Mrs. Edmonds warned us not say anything bad to him about her or we would be sorry, because as far as she was concerned she was treating us nice. And that is what we better say if he asked us. We changed into our school clothes and waited for the state man to arrive. Arnold was the lookout for him, and as soon as he saw him drive up he ran back into the house saying, "Here comes the state man." Mrs. Edmonds had us all sitting at the table in the kitchen all neat and smiling when he came into the house.

The state man introduced himself to us and asked us how we were doing. We all hoped that this would be the day that he would tell us that we would be leaving the Edmondses. We dared not tell him what was going on here, because if we did we knew that we would get the beating of our lives, and probably be executed and buried in the woods and never heard from again! Mrs. Edmonds told him that we were nice boys and that we were a happy family, and that we never got into any trouble. If only he could look into our eyes and see the agony and anguish in them. As he was asking us questions, I kept looking at Mrs. Edmonds each time he asked a question and she would give us threatening glares behind the state man's back. The state man noticed the nervous glances that I made to Mrs. Edmonds each time he asked a question. He asked Mrs. Edmonds if it would be all right if he could talk to us in private. She agreed and left the room. We knew that she didn't go too far and that she could hear us from the other room. We told him that everything was fine and we were happy to be here. Even Tony agreed that we were a happy family. He asked us if we were being fed properly and if she spanked us a lot. We said Mrs. Edmonds gave us a lot to eat and she hardly ever spanked us.

We lied and said she took us to the movies all the time. We lied a lot about how we were being treated because we knew that she was listening. I think the state man suspected that we were lying when he asked us questions regarding the treatment we received from the Edmondses because of the way we were nervously fidgeting around in our chairs when he asked certain questions.

Finally, after what seemed like an eternity, he said, "Okay, fellas, I want to talk with Mrs. Edmonds. I'll see you before I go." He then asked Mrs. Edmonds too accompany him into the living room so they could talk. We were in the kitchen and we could here Mrs. Edmonds talking in a loud voice. It sounded like the state man was upsetting her about something. Both of them sounded like they were arguing about something. We tried eavesdropping to hear what was being said. It sounded like Mrs. Edmonds was saying that those people were lying to her. We all wondered what people she was referring to. We could tell that she was mad at the state man. She told him that he shouldn't accuse her of something that was not true. We couldn't hear everything being said but could tell that it was not a pleasant conversation. We sat in silence and waited for them to finish. We hoped that he could detect that we were lying about everything. Whatever it was he told her made her very unhappy, and we knew that when he left we would probably get beaten. A few minutes later they came out of the other room and the state man said to us that he would be back again to check up on us. With that, he left.

As soon as the state man left, Mrs. Edmonds marched into the kitchen where we were and asked us in a stern voice what did we said to the state man, because he told her that he felt that we were not telling him the truth about how we were being treated. We told her that we told the state man that we liked it here. Tony said, "We didn't tell him anything bad about you; we told him that you treated us good."

She said, "You best have!" At least we didn't get the beating that we anticipated. She then made us change out of our clothes back into our rags and sent us scurrying "down back." We all went down back and sat in our circle and talked about the state man, saying things like, "I hope he comes back real soon and takes us away."

Tony talked about running away again.

Chapter 14

Camp Russell

Every summer the D.C.G. would send us to a summer camp called Camp Russell in Richmond, Massachusetts. The D.C.G. tried to get us in a boys' club camp in Williamstown, Massachusetts, but most of the time it was full, and the D.C.G. wanted us in a camp with a versatile environment, so it was off to Camp Russell. There we had a lot of fun. We had our own cabins, with a counselor for each cabin. Our counselor's name was Jack Nivens, a swell guy. He taught us how to swim, he took us on hikes, and we went fishing and played all kind of sports. At night we used to roast marshmallows by the campfire and Jack would tell us spooky stories, scaring us half to death. It was a lot of fun. This lasted for two weeks and then it was time to go "home." When that time came, all four of us became very despondent. We all knew where we were going. All of the other kids were singing camp songs and playing with each other while we four boys sat on the camp bus in silence wishing that we didn't have to go back to the

Edmondses. Tony took it harder than the rest of us. He really liked Camp Russell and wanted to go back. That's all he talked about for a week. He probably had found some kids there that were cowboy fans and that liked playing cowboys and Indians with him!

When we got back "home," Mrs. Edmonds didn't waste any time making us change our clothes and sending us "down back." There was no, "Hi, fellas! How was camp?" or, "Did you have a good time?" When we gathered together back "down back" we all sat in our little circle and spent the rest of the day talking about Camp Russell, wishing that we were still there and not here, "down back." We were all getting older and things weren't getting any better for us. Arnold and I were twelve years old, Michael was ten, and Tony was fifteen and becoming more and more rebellious towards the Edmondses, especially Mrs. Edmonds.

Uncle Charlie was still taking Arnold to the kiln to "help out." Mrs. Edmonds kept beating Michael and me for trivial things. She tried desperately to have Tony removed from the home because it was becoming more and more difficult for her to handle him. She knew that he had a lot of influence on us, and that made her very uncomfortable. We all felt that someday something was going to happen between Mrs. Edmonds and Tony, and finally one day it did.

It happened on a day when we were playing down back. Mrs. Edmonds came outside and stood with her hands on her hips. She called Tony to come up from down back. Tony said, "I wonder what she wants now." We could hear her yelling at Tony about going after Herbie with a big stick. I guess Herbie finally told her about the watch

88

incident that had happened a few months ago. She shouted at Tony, telling him that she should have him locked up for threatening Herbie. Tony tried to explain to her that Herbie was beating on us for no reason at all. Mrs. Edmonds did not want to hear any explanations; she picked up her board that she beat us with and in a threatening gesture raised it as if to hit Tony with it.

Suddenly Tony turned and dashed out of the driveway, running down Cole Avenue. Mrs. Edmonds called out to him and said, "Tony, get your butt back here right now!" But Tony was long gone. Mrs. Edmonds turned and went into the house. I guess she went in to call the "state people" and tell them that Tony ran away again.

While she was in the house Tony suddenly reappeared and sauntered back down back with us. Mrs. Edmonds looked out of the kitchen window and saw Tony back in the woods with us. She came back outside and called Tony, telling him to come to the house right now! Tony walked back up to where she was standing, waiting for her to start screaming at him again. But she didn't. Instead she said in a whisper, "I called the state people on you 'cause I'm sick and tired of you. I'm sick and tired of all of you. Now get out of here." She was real mad. I had never seen her so mad. Tony was mad too. He turned and walked back to where we were. He sat down on the heater with a real mean look on his face. I don't know what it was that he was thinking but I could tell it wasn't good.

The D.C.G. called Mrs. Edmonds a couple of days later and told her that they were going to try to find another home for Tony and to try to be patient with us, because we weren't bad boys, we just needed some love, understanding, and guidance.

Chapter 15

Hot Chicken Feet Soup and Hot Baths

Every now and then when it rained and Mrs. Edmonds was in one of her real bad moods, she would make us go outside in the rain in our underwear with a bar of soap and tell us to wash ourselves. Sometimes the rain would be cold, but she didn't care. One day while we were bathing in the rain, Herbie came outside and picked up a handful of dirt and threw it at us. Then he ran behind Arnold and me and slammed our heads together again.

We all dreaded "bath nights," those nights Mrs. Edmonds would force all four of us to bath into the same water, two at a time. She would force us to scrub each other with a thick, yellow-bristle scrub brush. If we didn't scrub hard enough, she would bend over in the tub and scrub us until our skin became raw. She made sure that the bath water was kept extremely hot. It would be so hot Michael would cry and beg her not to make him get into the tub. She would threaten him, telling him that he better get his butt in the tub or she would beat the dirt off of him. Poor Michael would stick his foot in the water and jerk it out in pain, crying. I would already be in the tub, telling him, "It's not so bad, Michael, come on." He would be screaming and splashing the hot water all over me and himself. After a short time our bodies would become numb from the water. Mrs. Edmonds told us that she wanted to make sure that we were clean.

Mrs. Edmonds seldom cooked meals. Uncle Charlie did most of the cooking. His favorite was homemade baked beans with molasses. Most of The the meals that Mrs. Edmonds did cook we ate without any problems, although they weren't as good as Uncle Charlie's, probably because we were starving anyway!

One day we were having a dinner that Mrs. Edmonds had prepared. I guess it was her favorite, because she cooked it almost every other day. It was chicken feet soup and it tasted awful. I don't think she ever washed the chicken feet before cooking them. She would boil the chicken feet in salt water with the yellow skin still on them. Then she would pour the "slop" in bowls and demand that we eat it or go to bed without anything at all. We could see the yellow feet floating around in the water with the potatoes that she boiled with them.

As we sat there looking at the bowl, Tony, Michael, and me managed to eat what was in it. Arnold started getting sick from it. He told Mrs. Edmonds that he couldn't eat any more of it. She raised her voice at him and told him that he'd better eat it or else. So Arnold tried to eat the rest of it, but ended up vomiting it up. When Mrs. Edmonds saw that, she slapped Arnold on the back of his head and told him to eat the mess that he made, meaning his own vomit. She had a habit of doing that with all of us at the table when she got mad at us if we didn't like what she cooked. She couldn't cook worth a damn. Sometimes she would just chase us away from the table and make us go back outside or to bed without any supper at all.

I don't know why Mrs. Edmonds always picked on me. I felt as though she hated me. Each time I "messed up," she would pick up the board that she used to beat us with and start beating me. I can't put into words the pain that I suffered with those beatings, not to mention that I was skin and bones; there was no meat bulk to soften the blows. Three or four times a week she would find a reason to beat Arnold and me with that board. I was terrified of her especially when she got "mad" at me. She would call me all kinds of names like "sloppy Joe" and "nappy head" and "stupid and useless." More than once she told me that I would never amount to anything. It got to the point to where I started believing her. I felt that she really didn't like me and wanted me to leave. I don't know what it was about me that she didn't like. I wish that I could do something to show her that I was a good boy, maybe make something in school for her.

There were times that I was sent to bed without supper and my stomach would hurt from the hunger pangs. Eventually I would cry myself to sleep until Tony or another one of my brothers brought me some food to eat.

Chapter 16

Rusty

Color TVs came into existence about 1953. The Evanses had one, and every now and then Mrs. Edmonds would allow us to go in to the living room and watch it. Of course, we had to sit on the floor. (God forbid we sit on the couch!) We used to watch *The Lone Ranger and Tonto, Sky King,* and *The Texas Rangers.* Watching TV was not something we did a lot of. Once every blue moon, Mrs. Edmonds allowed us to watch TV. Most of the time, it would be on Saturday mornings. Other than that, if it was a rainy day and we couldn't go outside, we had to sit on the floor in the pantry and listen to it and try to figure out what show was on, and we would try to follow it just by listening, like those old radio programs.

Each day we could hear the radio in the kitchen, and there was not one day that I didn't hear "How Much is That Doggie in the Window?" I forget who sang that song, but I know that she wasn't singing about Rusty. Rusty was the Edmondses' pet collie. He was a beautiful dog with gold and white fur. He was an amazing animal. He has been a part of the Edmonds family for a long time. And I guess he felt as though he had his rights. He was up there in age and spent most of his time lying under the kitchen table. But Rusty had a bad habit, and that was he loved to release gas! Fart! He farted a lot! Man, did he stink! Every evening at suppertime while we were sitting on the floor waiting to be fed, along with Rusty, we smelled an awful odor. It took us a while to figure out where the smell originated. Every time Rusty farted we got scolded and blamed for it. What a God-awful smell. A dog fart is one of the worst odors around.

One bad habit that Uncle Charlie had was feeding Rusty leftover food off of the table. One evening Uncle Charlie made some delicious homemade baked beans with molasses. I have to admit they were good. Like always after supper, Uncle Charlie fed Rusty the leftovers and all hell broke loose in the kitchen. Baked beans had the same effect on Rusty as they did on us. Uncle Charlie started yelling at us about farting in the house. We tried to explain to Uncle Charlie that it was his dog that was farting, but Uncle Charlie refused to accept the fact that his dog Rusty was a farting dog, period! Eventually the beans took their toll on us too, and as hard as we tried to refrain from farting we couldn't hold back any longer. We knew that if Uncle Charlie found out that we were the guilty ones now, he would have a fit.

Anyway the war was on between the four of us and Rusty. Poor Rusty couldn't take it any longer. He gave up, jumped up whimpering, scratching on the door, trying to get outside into the fresh air. Uncle Charlie came into the kitchen and opened the door for Rusty and then turned to us and asked us what was going on and who was bothering Rusty. We told him Rusty farted and couldn't stand his own fart. Uncle Charlie didn't think that was funny at all. He said, "My dog does not fart, it's you guys, and I'm not going to tell you anymore." A short time later Rusty came back into the house, and as he lay down in his usual spot I could have sworn that the look he gave us was like, "You guys had better stop farting around or else I will bite the crap' out of you, and I mean it! This is my spot, I've been here many years, way before you guys got here, and I ain't leaving it, so knock it off!"

Right about then Tony let loose with a "blast." I thought to myself, *We are in for it now*. We all wanted to gang up on Tony but the smell backed us off. Tony was older and his farts were older too.

Chapter 17

What Is a Holiday?

"*Trick or treat!*" For some strange reason Mrs. Edmonds let us go trick or treating in the neighborhood, probably to let the neighbors know how nice of a person she was! We would dress up in homemade costumes, and, of course, Tony was the Lone Ranger. His costume consisted of a black mask covering his eyes like the Loner Ranger. Michael was Tonto: he wore a homemade headband with a feather and face paint. Arnold was Roy Rogers and I was Superman. I had on a blue T-shirt with a homemade cape sticking out of the back.

On this particular night all four of us set out to collect some goodies. We went from house to house saying, "Trick or treat!" We were having a ball going from house to house. Some of the houses that we went to, the people would slam the door in our faces; others would tell us that they didn't have anything for us. That didn't stop us, though. Most of the people in the neighborhood were kind to us and gave us a lot of candy and apples. We knew that we had to be back home by a certain time, so after about an hour of trick-or-treating we went home with our bags full of candy. Herbie was in the front room watching TV. He told us to put our bags on the counter so that he could check them for us.

After leaving the bags of candy on the counter we went and sat down on the floor in the pantry, waiting for Herbie to give us our candy. He went through all of the bags and took candy and fruits out and put some of it in his pockets. We all looked at him wondering when he was going to give us the candy back. After taking what he wanted he went back into the living room to watch TV and eat candy. We looked at each other wondering what he was going to do. After a short time the Edmondses returned home, and as soon as they entered the house Herbie dashed out of the living room and told Mrs. Edmonds that we were late coming home from trick-or-treating, and that we tried to sneak into the house but he caught us. Mrs. Edmonds looked at us and asked us if that was true.

Tony said, "No, Miz. Edmonds, we came home when we were supposed to."

Herbie came over and stood over us and in a threatening gesture asked, "Tony, are you calling me a liar?"

Tony said, "No, but we did come home when we were supposed to." Mrs. Edmonds believed Herbie and turned and walked over to the counter where our bags were and took them off of the counter and dumped them in the trash. she She then dumped cooking grease on top of it so that we couldn't sneak behind her back and retrieve it later.

She said, "When you guys learn to get home on time when somebody lets you go somewhere, then you can have the things that you get." Herbie was in the living room snickering. We didn't think it was funny at all. Tony tried to explain to Mrs. Edmonds that Herbie was lying, but she believed him and that was that. She told us to be quiet and that Herbie had no reason to lie. The rest of us just sat there. Michael had tears in his eyes and Arnold and Tony were mad as hell. I couldn't believe what Herbie did. I think it was planned all along between Mrs. Edmonds and Herbie to take our candy anyway; she only let us go trick-or-treating just to impress the neighbors. She had no intention of letting us keep the Halloween candy. Later when we all were in the bedroom getting ready for bed, Arnold and Tony reached inside their pants pockets and pulled out a handful of candy each. I guess when we were out doing the trick-or-treating thing they were putting candy in their pockets. They gave Michael and me some of it and we went to bed eating Halloween candy. We were *tricked* but as least we had a little *treat,* thanks to Tony and Arnold.

Thanksgiving is a holiday when families get together to give thanks for what they have. The Edmondses, like other families, served a big Thanksgiving dinner with all of the trimmings. Various family members would come with all sorts of dishes. They would all sit in the dining room and enjoy their feast, laughing and talking, basically having a good time. We did not have much to laugh and talk about, but I must admit they gave us more food to eat than they normally do. We had turkey, ham, chicken (not the feet), fresh garden vegetables, mashed potatoes, the works. It's a day when people give thanks for what they have; it's also a day when people "pig out."

There is one Thanksgiving Day that I find hard to forget. It was a nice warm day in November. It had snowed the night before. All four of us were anticipating the Thanksgiving feast that was being prepared in the house. A lot of the Edmondses' relatives came over to help with the cooking. We were waiting for that knock on the window so that we could go inside and gobble up that Thanksgiving dinner that the Edmondses were preparing. We decided to kill some time by making a snow fort.

After we completed the fort, we started bombarding each other with snowballs. As I turned around to get some more "ammo," suddenly *bam!*—I didn't know what hit me. It felt like an ice glacier. Man, was I mad. I turned around to see who it was that blasted me with that "ice ball" (an ice ball is a snowball packed real hard; it's like a block of ice). It hurts like hell when you get hit by one. Arnold was standing there laughing his butt off while making another ice ball to "launch" at me. I remembered the needle incident before when I told on him. I knew that I couldn't tell on him again. That made me angrier, so I mustered up as much courage as I could and ran up to Arnold and pushed him down into the snow. He got back up and pushed me back in anger. The fight was on.

Tony and Michael didn't try to stop us; they just stood there watching. After a few minutes of rolling around in the snow, the knock on the window finally came. We stopped fighting, brushed ourselves off, and filed into the house. I guess Mrs. Edmonds was watching us from the window, because as soon as we entered the house she looked at Arnold and me and asked us what we were fighting about.

I said, "We were not fighting, we were just playing." As we were talking I observed the other family members sitting around the dinner table in the dining room waiting to get started on their feast. A couple of them were watching Mrs. Edmonds and us in curiosity. The food smelled and looked good. I could see a big turkey with all of the trimmings, and a big ham with cranberry sauce. They had everything that you could imagine. The works.

Mrs. Edmonds asked us again why we were fighting. Again I answered and said that "we were not fighting, we were just playing."

Mrs. Edmonds wasn't buying that story. She looked at the both of us and said, "If you don't tell me the truth, I am going to whip the both of you, do you hear me?" I didn't want another whipping, so as I looked at Tony and Arnold. I knew that I had no choice. I didn't want another beating. So in a soft voice I told Mrs. Edmonds that we were fighting because Arnold threw an ice ball at me and I got mad.

She said, "Speak up!"

I said, "We were fighting because Arnold threw a snowball at me!"

She asked, "Why didn't you tell me that in the first place? How many times have I told you about fighting?" She then turned to Tony and asked him why he didn't stop us from fighting. I thought to myself that this was supposed to be a Thanksgiving holiday. Why was she yelling at us? Tony said that he thought we were just playing around; that's why he didn't try to stop us. I told her that I didn't want to tell the truth because I didn't want to get Arnold into trouble. She stared at the both of us for a minute then motioned for us to go sit and wait for dinner.

As we sat on the floor in the pantry, I couldn't look my brothers in the eyes; I felt that they were angry with me again for being a tattletale. This time I was wrong. Tony said, "Don't worry about it, man, we understand."

Mrs. Edmonds came back into the pantry where we were and said, "Go wash up and get to the table." We rushed into the bathroom washed our hands and face and sat down at the table, waiting for our feast. The rest of the family was already eating their food. As we sat waiting we talked in low voices and made a few smart remarks to each other. Mrs. Edmonds came into the kitchen carrying two plates full of food. She sat one down in front of Tony and the other in front of Arnold. Both plates were loaded with turkey, ham, string beans, cranberry sauce, corn on the cob, stuffing, and gravy. Wow! Even Arnold's plate was full, and that was unusual.

Mrs. Edmonds came back from the kitchen with two more plates. She sat one down in front of Michael; his plate was stacked with delicious Thanksgiving food. When she sat my plate down in front of me, I looked down into it and couldn't believe what I saw. There was only a slice of bread with gravy and an ear of corn on my plate. Mrs. Edmonds looked at me and said, "When you learn to tell me the truth when I ask you a question then I will treat you like everybody else!"

I looked at her and said, "Yes, Miz Edmonds. I'm sorry. Can I have some more food?" She gave me a mean look and turned and walked back into the dining room, where the rest of her family was feasting and stuffing themselves.

Tears welled up in my eyes. This was her idea of punishment. I knew that I was going to start crying. My feelings were hurt. Tony and Arnold put their hands on my shoulders and said, "Sorry, man." They tried to console me. The next thing I knew Arnold started taking food from his plate and putting it on mine. I guess he was looking out for his twin brother. Michael and Tony did the same thing. Most of the time they would be taking food from my plate, but this time it was different. I really started crying then.

I had three brothers to be thankful for on Thanksgiving.

Christmas was a day when children couldn't wait to get up in the morning and open gifts. I can't remember ever doing that. We had no gifts. The Edmondses treated us as outcasts on Christmas Day. We spent most of the day down back in the woods in the snow. The rest of the family spent the day inside opening gifts and basically having a good time with each other. A lot of family members brought gifts over to the house and placed them under the tree. None of them had our names on them. I remember looking under the tree and seeing a mountain of presents under it. None of them were ours, with the exception of a few gifts given to us by the D.C.G. The Edmondses had us pose under the tree for photos. I guess they were trying to impress the state man when he came to visit us during the Christmas holidays. We were all sitting in front of the tree smiling as if we were the happiest kids on the block! We did our own Christmas shopping at the South Street Market and Boyd's Market, and a few other stores on North Street. If we got lucky we would find a store full of Christmas toys and play Santa Claus with each other. I remember shortly after the holidays, one day while we were walking to school, an older white lady stopped us and asked us if we enjoyed the cookies that she made for us. We looked at each other wondering what she was talking about.

Tony said, "We never got any cookies." She said that she gave them to her son to bring over to the Edmondses for us. I guess the cookies never made it to us.

(Back Row) Alex, Tony, Arnold,

(Front Row) Michael at Christmas in Pittsfield

(Courtesy of Gary A. Gaulin)

Easter is a holiday that celebrates the resurrection of Christ. It is also a time when people dress up in their new Easter outfits and attend church services. Easter egg hunting was a fun thing for kids, but we never had the opportunity to go to any Easter egg hunts. Mrs. Edmonds sent us to church on Easter Sunday. It was the First Baptist Church on North Street; it was a big church. We did not have Easter suits to wear to church; we wore our school clothes.

In church the four of us sat in a pew in the back. There we laughed and joked around, making noise and punching each other. Every now and then an older white lady who was sitting in the pew in front of us turned around and put her fingers to her lips, telling us to be quiet. We did for a few minutes then Tony would start making jokes and calling one of us a funny name, then we would start snickering and whispering and fidgeting in our seats. Arnold would punch me or Michael then Michael would say, "Stop hitting me, man," and again the old lady would turn in her seat and tell us to be quiet. I'm sure in her mind she was thinking, "What a noisy bunch of little *colored* boys. I sure wish that they would shut up!" And why were we in her church anyway?

Finally when the services were over and when we were on our way out, the little old lady who kept telling us to be quiet came up to us and said "You boys should be ashamed of yourselves you should know better that to play around in church. I should tell your mother, but I won't because it's Easter."

We all answered her, saying, "Yes, ma'am we're sorry," and walked away laughing. When we got back home, Mrs. Edmonds made us change our clothes and sent us down back. There we had our own

Easter egg hunt. We made fake Easter eggs out of pine cones and then we would hide them from each other. That was basically how we celebrated Easter.

It was Friday the weekend of Mother's Day, and school was almost over. I was anxious to get out when the teacher said, "All right, class, before you go home today I want you to make some nice Mother's Day cards to bring home to your mothers, okay?" She then handed out some crayons and coloring paper. I spent a considerable amount of time making a Mother's Day card for Mrs. Edmonds, hoping that she might like me for making it for her.

When I completed the card, the teacher looked at it and said, "Alexander this is a very nice card. Your mother will love it." I felt proud of what I had done. I couldn't wait to bring it home and give it to Mrs. Edmonds. I felt like she didn't like me, so I figured if I give her a nice card she might like me.

After school while walking home with my brothers, I showed them the card that I had made. Tony looked at it and said, "She ain't gonna like it."

I said, "Yes she will." I was very excited. I couldn't wait to see the look on Mrs. Edmonds' face when I gave her the card.

When we got home I ran in the house, and while holding the card behind my back I said, "Miz Edmonds, I got something for you." She was sitting in the living room reading a magazine. She looked at me and asked me what it was that I had. I handed her the card, telling her that I made it especially for her.

She looked at it then at me and put the card on the coffee table and said, "Don't just stand there—don't you have chores to do? Get going." She then went back to reading the magazine.

I stood there for a moment, stunned. I thought at least she would say thank you or something, but she just sat there reading the magazine. She raised her head and looked at me as if to say, "What are you waiting for? Go!" She then waved me away. So I went to my room, changed my clothes, and after finishing my chore of cleaning the chicken coop, I went down back and told my brothers what happened.

Tony said, "I told you."

Michael said, "Maybe she was in a bad mood. Maybe she will like it later." I still had hopes that maybe she would say, "Thank you, Alex, for the beautiful Mother's Day card," and maybe give me a big hug at dinnertime. A couple of hours later we heard the knock on the window and went into the house, and as usual we sat on the floor. While we were sitting there waiting to eat, I looked across the room and saw my Mother's Day card that I had made for Mrs. Edmonds all crumpled up in the trashcan. My feelings were hurt. My eyes started watering. I was ready to cry.

Tony put his hand on my shoulder and said in his usual Western drawl, "Alex, man, I liked your card. I think it was great. I don't care what Mrs. Edmonds says." This was one of those times that I wanted so desperately to see my real mother. I know how she would have felt when I gave her the card. I know that she would have said, "Thank you, son. I love you very much."

Chapter 18

"Aunt Jamama"

I can't remember ever seeing any other colored people in Pittsfield when we were little, with the exception of one day while we were on our way to Clapp Park. We decided to stop in a grocery store and do a little "shopping." While we were standing in the aisle trying to figure out how we were going to "shop," a very large colored lady came down the aisle pushing a shopping cart full of groceries. She stopped in front of us. Holy cow was she fat! She was bigger than Edith Edmonds. Her hair was real short and her lips were on the large side.

She asked us, "What is y'all young 'uns doin' in here? And where is y'all's momma? I sho' hope that y'all ain't stealin' nuttin'! 'Cause stealin' makes us colored people look bad."

I couldn't help wondering how anybody could make her look any worse than she already looked. She talked funny. I'd never heard the word "y'all." We told her that we were going to buy some candy and cupcakes. She stood there looking at us. I know she didn't believe us. Tony was about to say something to her.

As she kept talking to us, I kept staring at a box of pancake mix that was sitting on the shelf right behind her. I saw a picture of a colored lady on the front of the box that looked just like the lady that was talking to us. I started to ask her if that was her picture on the front of the box but I changed my mind. On the front of the box it said "Aunt Jamima" or "Jamama" or something like that. Suddenly an older white lady came over to us and asked the colored lady what was taking her so long.

The big colored lady said, "I'm ready, ma'am." She then sauntered down the aisle behind the white lady, and she kind of reminded me of an elephant the way she walked. We left the store empty-handed and went on to the park, laughing at big Aunt. "Jamama"

A few days later, while we were on the way to the movies in downtown Pittsfield, we decided to stop at a store called J.J. Newberrys on North Street. We were going to pick up a few items to take to the movies to munch on. As we entered the store we saw a whole lot of colored people sitting at the lunch counter, but they weren't eating. So Tony, being the nosey person that he was, asked a colored lady what was going on. She told him that they were protesting for civil rights and that this was a "sit-in" for equal rights for the colored people.

I guess these were Pittsfield's colored people demonstrating for equal rights. We decided this would not be a good day to pick up anything, so we left empty-handed. After all, how would it look, four colored boys caught stealing from a store filled with colored people especially after what "Aunt "Jamama said about us making colored people look bad?

I didn't know until years later that there were a lot of colored people living on the north side of town in Pittsfield. I never saw them prior to the "sit-in." We lived on the south side of town, which was predominantly white.

We had heard that there were a lot of colored people lived in Springfield, Massachusetts, and that it was bad place to live.

Chapter 19

Leaving "Down Back"

Tony ran away again. Only this time someone did something about it. Later on that same day that Tony ran away and was brought back, Mrs. Edmonds called us all into the house. Imagine that! She actually verbally called us into the house, not the usual knock on the window. We all thought that she was going to beat Tony in front of us so as to discourage us from thinking about running away with Tony.

As we filed into the house we automatically went over to our little corner in the pantry to sit on the floor, but Mrs. Edmonds stopped us and told us to sit at the table because she had something to tell us. *Something is definitely wrong,* I thought. *She has never been this nice to us since we've been here.* She went on to tell us that she received a call from the state people, and they informed her that they found a new foster home for us. A place called Springfield.

We had heard about Springfield. We heard that it was a big city and a bad place to live. Their intention was to remove us from her care in a week. She did not want that to happen but she couldn't stop it. She said that she didn't want to see us go and that she would miss us. Once again some of the new words and I learned at Clapp Park came into my mind and those were, "You're full of shit!" She then told us we could go into the front room and watch TV until suppertime. We were all in shock. Speechless.

After supper we went back to the living room and watched some more TV. After a couple of hours, Mrs. Edmonds sent us to bed. We all had a stomach full of food. Arnold was in high spirits as were Tony and the rest of us. We were so excited. Finally we were getting out of here, unless Mrs. Edmonds was lying to us. Maybe she was trying to trick us, for what reason I don't know.

Tony said, "We better watch out 'cause she may be lying. But if she isn't then we finally will be getting out of here. I guess somebody read my letter."

Letter? What letter? we asked. Tony said that he wrote a letter one day while he was in school and gave it to his teacher to read. He said maybe she gave it to the state people.

That night while in bed, we took a chance and started talking like normal kids in bed, and no one came into our room to beat us to sleep. It was a strange feeling. Arnold's stomach was full of food and he was elated, as we all were.

A week later the "four boys" were packed and sitting at the kitchen table for the last time. "Uncle Charlie" was standing near the sink. He had a strange look on his face. If I didn't know any better I would say it was fear. Edith was sitting at the table wearing her nurse's uniform, trying to smile. I know it must have hurt her to do it. She always scared me. Mrs. Edmonds was sitting at the table telling us how she enjoyed having us and how much she would miss us. And all we could say was, "Yes, Miz Edmonds."

Eventually the state man arrived. After a brief conversation, we loaded our tied-together suitcases in the state man's car. Mrs. Edmonds came out to the car, pretending to be heartbroken. She was full of baloney! She said, "I hope you boys will come back to see me someday."

As we were driving down Cole Avenue, Arnold, Michael, and me were in the backseat and Tony was in the front with the state man. I could see the sun's rays glistening on the leaves of the maple trees that lined the sidewalk on Cole Avenue. We were finally leaving the Edmondses for good. I saw the trash cans that we used to rummage through, neatly lined up along the tree line. I hoped that no other kids would ever have to dig in them to find food to eat like we did. I thought about old Abigail Hackleberry. I'm sure she won't miss us. I wonder what the big colored lady "Aunt " "Jamama" was doing right about now. Probably in another store, walking around like an elephant following the white lady around, worrying about us making colored people look bad.

As we were driving along I thought about Officer Haskell the friendly, fat policeman. I will miss him. I was glad that we were getting away from the mean detective because he frightened me. The morning air was crisp and fresh. All four of us sat in silence. It was a very strange feeling leaving the Edmondses for good, but a good feeling leaving "down back" forever! It was 1957.

"Somewhere over the rainbow skies are blue, and the dreams that you dare to dream really do come true."

Chapter 20

Next Stop

All four of us were a little nervous about where we were going. The state man said, "You fellas will like Springfield and your new foster parents." I must have dozed off while he was talking, because when I woke up I saw a lot of big buildings and stores. The state man said that we were in downtown Springfield, Massachusetts. I woke up the rest of my brothers pointing and shouting.

"Wow! Look at those big buildings and all those people." This place didn't look anything like Pittsfield. Wow! There were a lot of stores and movie theatres. As we got closer to our new home, I saw a whole lot of colored people. I had never seen that many colored people in one place in my life! They were all around. There were a lot of colored kids our age playing in the street and in their yards, riding bicycles, and chasing each other around. It looked like Springfield was all colored people. Maybe that was why Mrs. Edmonds didn't want us to come here, because she had heard that Springfield was a dangerous place to live with all those colored people.

We turned down a long street and pulled up in front of a big house. This was our new home on Northampton Avenue in Springfield, Massachusetts. Our new foster parents came out and helped the state man bring our tied-together suitcases in the house. The state man introduced us to them, and they introduced themselves to us as Mr. and Mrs. Woodbury. They talked funny. I'd never heard that kind of talking before. It was real fast; I could hardly understand what they were saying. Later I found out that they were called Jamaican people. We followed them into the house and met their other two children, Jamie and Earl. The father, Mr. Woodbury, was tall and slightly bald and wore glasses. Mrs. Woodbury was short and heavy. She had a rather large set of lips. And her nose entered a room way before the rest of her body. It was quite large.

Mrs. Woodbury showed us to our room in the attic. The state man talked for a few minutes with the Woodburys, telling them that he would be back from time to time to check on us. He shook hands with each one of us then he was gone.

The Woodburys were very strict but not as mean as the Edmondses. Whenever we did something wrong, Mrs. Woodbury would beat us, and while she was doing that she would be shouting in Jamaican at us, asking why we had done whatever it was she was whipping us for. Between the pain of the lashing and the language barrier, it was tough to answer her. She would get angrier with us, thinking that we were trying to be smart. But it wasn't that; we just couldn't understand her with that Jamaican accent.

Whenever we were confined to our attic bedroom we used to send Arnold out the window to sneak to the corner store and get us some candy. The way we did it, we would have Arnold climb out the window and shimmy down the water spout then we would watch for him to return. When we saw him running back down the street, Tony would run downstairs and open the door to the common hallway, which led up to the third floor. He never got caught.

Homer Street School was the first school that I went to in Springfield. Tony went to a school called Springfield Trade High School. He was constantly being sent home from school for bad behavior. I think Tony was ready to quit school, because he kept getting into trouble. He didn't care about school anymore. He kept talking about quitting school and going into the service. I was still getting bad report cards. School and me didn't get along either.

Mrs. Woodbury would get in a bad mood from time to time and beat one of us for something trivial. She didn't like Arnold at all. She used to pick on him all the time. There were times when Mrs. Woodbury would yell at Arnold, and the neighbors would hear her and yell at her from their yards, telling her to "leave that boy alone."

One lady we used to call Miss Shirley lived down the street from us. Every now and then when the Woodburys were out shopping or whatever, she would take us in her house and feed us snacks and juice. She let us watch her TV until Mrs. Woodbury came home. She was nice; she didn't like the way Mrs. Woodbury treated us.

Mrs. Woodbury had a leather belt that she used, and when she used it she would hit us with extreme force. Sometimes I think that she regretted taking us in. I don't remember seeing her ever beat any of her kids. She did allow us to go out and play in the park across the street, a small park called Gunn Square. We used to play with both white kids and colored kids. I remember one day while Arnold and me were cutting through the park, a bunch of white kids started chasing us. Both of us ran like hell. One of the white kids threw a knife at me. Thank God he missed.

Another time while playing in Gunn Square, my brother Michael got into a fight with a colored boy named Billy. It looked like Billy was getting the best of Michael. He was a big boy. I don't know what got into me but suddenly I found myself running across the park to where they were. I jumped up in the air and kicked Billy in the head, knocking him to the ground. He jumped up and took off across the park. I actually thought that he was going to get up and beat the crap out of me; after all, I was only 130 pounds—a scarecrow. But thank God he just turned and ran. We were all getting older and meaner I guess.

Our new state man, Mr. Gibbons, came to visit us a couple of times. He would ask us how things were going. We would tell him everything was fine. At least things weren't as bad as they were in Pittsfield with the Edmondses.

I honestly can't remember celebrating any holidays at the Woodburys. Like the Edmondses, on Christmas we never got any presents except from the state, and on Easter we would dress up in good clothes but nothing new. Mrs. Woodbury would always find a reason to yell at us. Mr. Woodbury seemed like a nice man. He never yelled at us; he would always sit us down and talk to us if we did something wrong. Unfortunately, I think that we took advantage of that and got out of control.

One day, Mr. Gibbons, our social worker, came to visit us and see how things were going. I guess Mrs. Woodbury took the opportunity to express her feelings about us to him. She explained to him that she thought we were going to be good boys and that we were not what she had expected.

She made it clear that she would like to have us removed as soon as possible. She told him that she couldn't handle us anymore. She said that she wanted some more kids in the future so she could show the Welfare Department that she could take care of foster kids. But she just couldn't handle us. Personally I don't think we were all that bad, outside of Arnold and Michael stealing all of the time. Arnold got caught more than once, and each time he would blame it on another kid, named Vincent, saying that Vincent put him up to it.

Personally I never met Vincent. I think he was a schoolmate that took advantage of Arnold. Anyway, arrangements were made to have us removed, so a year later we were uprooted again, off to another foster home. This time we were split up. Tony was placed with a family on Dorchester Street. There he stayed for a year before joining the Marines. Michael was placed with a family on Quincy Street for a year then placed with the same family that Tony had been with on Dorchester Street, after Tony went into the service. The Massachusetts

State Welfare Department conducted an equivalency test on Arnold prior to placing him in another foster home. In their opinion, they felt that his IQ was not up to standards for placement into another foster home. Consequently, he was placed in the Belchertown State School in Belchertown, Massachusetts. I was placed in another foster home on Pendleton Avenue with a family called the Docketts. The year was 1958.

"My twin brother Arnold"

Chapter 21

"If Happy Little Bluebirds Fly Beyond the Rainbow, Why Oh Why Can't I?"

Deacon Dockett

His hands were the size of baseball gloves, and when he hit me, my ears rang and my lips would bleed.

My new foster parents were Percival and Evelyn Dockett. They were God-fearing people. One would think I formed my own opinion about that! Percival was short and stocky; he was called "Percy" for short. He was bald and wore thin-rimmed glasses on his moon-shaped face. They made him look meaner than he already was. Evelyn was tall and freckle faced. Both of them were originally from North Carolina. Percy was a deacon at a Baptist church and Evelyn a deaconess.

We lived in a medium-sized three-story house on Pendleton Avenue. I was the only child there at first. Later three other foster kids were placed there with me. Mr. Dockett's hands were huge and when he hit me I knew I was hit! It didn't take much for that to happen. It seemed like Deacon Dockett loved to bang away on me every other day. If I screwed up on something that he had asked me to do, there would be no talking to me and explaining what it was that I had done wrong. It was just *pow!* right in my face, and then I'd get sent up to my room in the attic. That was my domain. I remember many evenings that I would sit by the small Victorian window in my attic bedroom, watching the other kids playing and listening to records outside in the street. I longed to be outside with them. They looked like they were having so much fun. But I was forbidden to go out and play with them.

The Docketts had a big vegetable garden in the backyard and it was my job to keep the weeds out of it, pick the vegetables, and generally do the harvesting. Another one of the duties that was "assigned" to me was to mow the lawn of an elderly gentleman that lived down the street from us. I remember every time he talked to me "spittle" would come from his mouth, hitting me in the face. It used to make me sick. I dreaded the thought of going over to his house each time. It was also my job to cut the grass in the churchyard two streets behind our house and trim the bushes around the Third Baptist Church on the corner. In the winter it was my job to shovel the sidewalk around the Third Baptist Church before the parishioners arrived. It would be so cold. I didn't have any gloves and my hands would get numb from the cold. I couldn't go into the house until I finished the job. It was a long sidewalk around the church and no one helped me. I was never allowed to ask why I had to do all of those chores; if I did I would be reprimanded and probably beaten by Deacon Dockett with his favorite board.

Every now and then they would let me go to the neighborhood playground called Barrows Playground, which was just down the street. I had a curfew, and God forbid I be late coming home from the playground. There I got the chance to meet other kids and play basketball with them. My park days were few and far between. I spent most of my time in the garden or painting the house, washing Deacon Dockett's car, or fixing whatever was broken around the house. I also spent a lot of time in the house polishing silverware and furniture after school.

A lot of the Docketts' relatives would come over and visit along with friends of the family. Most of them treated me nice. One particular couple who lived a few houses down the street from me, named George and Kitty White, treated me like their own son. Occasionally on a Sunday afternoon they would come over to the Docketts and take me with them and their kids to an amusement park called Mountain Park. There were a lot of rides and games in the park. I remember George would give me a handful of change and tell me go have fun. I loved him for that. I would run around the park like a maniac, not knowing where to begin. I would play lots of games. I didn't go on too many rides. I just liked playing all the games. When I ran out of money Mr. White would give me another handful of change, and off I was again. I hated the thought of going back to the Docketts at the end of the day.

I always wanted to live with George and Kitty White. They were nice people.

Another couple that used to treat me nice was Bernard and Rena. They used to come over a lot. I remember one day while I was in the bed sick with the flu, Bernard came up to my room and said, "Here, Alex, I brought you some Tang." It sounded like he said, "I brought you some*thing*"—that's how it sounded. Many times Bernard would sit and talk with me, telling me that everything was going to be all right some day. It made me feel good to know that somebody in this world cared about me. It's a shame that the people I was living with didn't show me the love and compassion that outsiders did. The only thing Deacon Percival Dockett ever gave me was a slap in the mouth. He gave me plenty of those.

There were these two brothers, Otis and Marvin, who used to come over and visit. I think they were relatives of Deacon Dockett. They were both "cool dudes." Otis was a little older than me and Marvin was two years younger than me. I envied them a lot. I knew that they lived in a nice house and probably never got beatings like I did. I could tell the way they always laughed and joked with each other that they were happy. Otis was very soft-spoken, tall, and good-looking, Marvin was a little shorter. He was a lot of fun. We used to go outside and he would try to teach me how to sing. He had a nice voice. He said that someday he was going to be a singer and have a singing group of his own.

I was baptized in the Third Baptist Church, and joined the church choir. Every Tuesday night we had choir practice. There was a pretty girl named Emma that used to sing in the choir. I had a teenage crush on her. She never knew it, though. I thought that she was the prettiest girl in town. I looked forward to seeing her every Tuesday night. The nights that she didn't come to practice I would be disappointed. I kept looking towards the door to see if maybe she might be coming in late. But as time went on, and the later it got, I resolved myself to the fact that Emma was not going to be at choir practice that night. I didn't feel like singing then and our choir director Mrs. Fullilove would snap at me and tell me to pay attention to what I was supposed to be singing.

There was another girl in church that I had a secret admiration for. Her name was Sandy. She was gorgeous. I liked her too. She had an older sister named Margaret who used to beat on me at church. She was bigger than me. I used to run away from her; I was only 130 pounds, soaking wet. Sandy's mother, Mrs. Wallace, kept a close watch on her. I can see why. She was a fox. I'm sure I wasn't the only kid that liked her. I was too shy to approach her and tell her that I was madly in love with her. So I kept my admiration to myself. The Docketts had a radio in the kitchen and when I was sentenced to hard labor in the house—washing dishes, polishing all of the silverware, and scrubbing the floors, polishing the furniture, and whatever else they could find for me to do—I used to sing along with some of the songs that I heard on the radio. One particular song that I liked was a song by the Shirelles, a 1950s female singing group. It was a song called "*This is Dedicated to the One I Love.*" I used to love that song. Every time I heard it I would think of Sandy and sing to myself, pretending that I was singing to her.

Every summer the Docketts would sponsor a church picnic in their backyard. Mrs. Dockett would be in the kitchen cooking up a storm and the Deacon and I would be in the yard setting up picnic tables; and, of course, I was the one who cut the grass and pulled the weeds so the yard would look nice and neat for the church people. Other church members would bring food over and help out with the cooking. I remember the first picnic they had, I thought that since I was part of the family I could join everybody else, so I went into the yard, and before I knew it Deacon Dockett came up to me and with a real mean look on his face asked me what did I think I was doing coming out into the yard? I said that I thought that I could.

He said, "Get back inside the house right now!" I ran back inside the house up to my room. My feelings were hurt and I was afraid that Deacon Dockett was going to come inside after me and beat me for coming out into the yard with out his permission.

The only time I was allowed to come out was when they needed me to run back and forth to the store to pick up things that they ran out of. Other than that I had to stay in my room and look out the window at all of the church people eating and having fun. I wonder what the Docketts told them when they asked where I was. I couldn't understand why they didn't allow me to join everybody else.

I kept pretty much to myself and didn't make too many friends. There were a few kids that I became friends with. There was this one kid we used to call "Curky." His real name was Curtis Wilkerson. Curtis was a quiet kid very soft spoken boxing was one of his hobbies.

whenever someone mistook his quietness for weakness they found out the hard way that Curky was no pushover. He knew that a lot of kids used to pick on me because of my size he used to try to teach me how to box. There was another kid named James Bailey. We used to call him "Beetle Bailey." He was cool. He sang in the choir with me. All the girls in the choir used to say that James and I were the cutest boys in the choir—now that was questionable. If I was so cute how come I couldn't get a girlfriend? I guess maybe I might have been the cutest boy but also the "biggest square"!

Every now and then the Docketts would let me go over to James' house. His family welcomed me with open arms. His mom was an angel. His father was a minister. There were times that Reverend Bailey would sit down and talk with me, telling me not to worry because one day everything was going to be all right. He could see the anguish in my eyes. I guess he knew what I was going through.

James eventually went into the Marines and did a stint in Vietnam, where he was wounded in action and awarded a Purple Heart.

There was a couple of other kids that sang in the B.T.U. (Baptist Training Union) choir with me that I thought was cool one was a kid named George Philip Malone he was the choir clown. He was always telling corny jokes making people laugh .All of the girls liked him. There was one girl who used to call him "the kid" that used to make him mad as hell I guess it wa an ego thing. Another kid that had a beautiful voice was a boy named Leslie Anderson. Our choir director Mrs. Fullilove would have him sing a song called *"swing low sweet chariot"* and when he did he was awesome . I knew that with a voice like that he would go someplace some day he did – in later years he joined a renowned dowop 50's singing group called "**the dubs**" they are still performing to this day.

Another kid that I became very close to was a kid named Gus Stovall. We called him "Gussie." Gussie and I became real "tight." I used to go over to his house and "pig out." His mom was a great cook. After eating we would go to Barrows Playground and Gussie would try to teach me how to play basketball even though I was clumsy as hell. He had a lot of patience with me. Gussie used to chase all the girls around the playground, or they would chase him. For some strange reason they never chased me! I wonder why. He had two older brothers, Herschel and Warren, and a whole bunch of sisters. One in particular whose name was Beatrice was a tomboy. Every time I came to the house she would start punching on me trying to beat me up, which she almost did a few times.

Gussie and I would get into a little mischief from time to time. He had a BB gun and we used to sneak up to his room and shoot out of the window at squirrels and birds. Sometimes we would miss the squirrels and hit a window, at which time he would quickly stash the gun away as if nothing had happened, and we would go back to the park. On the way out I would innocently say, "Well, goodbye, Mrs. Stovall. I will see you tomorrow."

She would say, "Bye, Alex. You behave now, you hear?" I sure wished I could have lived with them. They were a nice family. The last time I saw Gussie we were just hanging around in the playground with some of the other guys, talking about what we were going to do after we got out of school. I remember asking Gussie what branch of the service he wanted to go in.

He said, "I am not sure yet. Between the Marines and the Army. How about you?"

I said, "I'm definitely going in the Marines, so I can wear the dress blue uniforms."

Another kid that was sitting with us laughed and said, "Aw man, you ain't gonna make it in the Marines! You're too skinny." That's the last time I saw Gussie.

Gussie eventually went into the Army. He was killed in Vietnam in March of 1967—I miss my buddy.

"Gussie"

(Courtesy of Hershel Stovall)

The winters at the Docketts' were brutal. Along with shoveling the church sidewalks, I was forced to go out when it was freezing and chop ice off of Percy's car. *"Alex, come inside and have a hot cup of hot chocolate."* You would think that someone with an ounce of compassion would say those words, but not the Docketts (the deacon or the deaconess). I was not allowed inside until I finished doing whatever Deacon Dockett ordered me to do, whether it was chopping ice off his car or chopping ice off the sidewalk in front of the house, or shoveling snow around the whole neighborhood.

Mr. Dockett had a mean streak in him that was unbelievable. To this day I can't imagine how the D.C.G. even considered the Docketts as decent foster parents. Those that knew him thought that he was a straight-up guy, being a deacon in church, saying amen every Sunday, and doing whatever things deacons do in church. I wonder if what he did to me one Sunday afternoon was "deacon-ish."

We were having a dinner and I had just finished drinking a glass of milk when I burped. It was rather loud. I didn't mean for it to happen; it just came out. Why did I do that? Deacon Dockett jumped up from the table and went to the refrigerator. He brought a gallon of milk back to the table and stood over me filling my empty glass back up. He then said, "Drink this right now!" I drank the whole glass of milk. He filled the glass up once again and ordered me to drink it. By now I was bloated and in no way could I drink any more. I told him that I couldn't drink any more. My stomach was hurting. He said, "You're going to drink this milk right now! Now drink it." Mrs. Dockett just sat there looking at us and said nothing. Mr. Dockett said in a threatening voice, "You better drink it or else!" I tried to drink some more but I couldn't. Mr. Dockett then slammed the gallon of milk down on the table and slapped me across the face. The slap was so hard it made Evelyn Dockett flinch. Then he told me to get away from the table until I learned some manners. I left what was remaining on my plate and went up to my room. My stomach and face were hurting bad and I was getting sick from all the milk Mr. Docket forced me to drink.

Deacon Dockett would beat me with his huge hands or whatever he could find at the time: a shoe, a strap, or a piece of wood from the basement. Many times he would start beating me on the second floor, and in my attempt to get away from him I would trip and fall down the stairs, but that didn't stop him. He would come after me and pound on me as I lay on the stairs cowering. There were times that he beat me so hard I would have bruises and welts all over my body. The more I cried in anguish the harder he beat me.

I had the pleasure of watching TV with them in the evening for an hour after I had completed my chores, as long as I sat there and kept my mouth shut. Percy would be sitting in his recliner with his feet up, chewing his Days Work tobacco and drinking his Coca-Cola. It was a ritual with him to send me to the store every day to get his Days Work chewing tobacco and a six-pack of Coca-Cola. While walking to the store, I saw other kids playing in the playground and wanted to be with them. They were having lots of fun, playing basketball and flirting with the girls. I used to run past the park real fast so no one would see me. My attire was not the greatest and I did not want to be the subject of schoolyard conversation among the other kids.

I remember attending Buckingham Junior High School. Buckingham Junior High was a school in the predominantly colored neighborhood. Just about every colored kid in Springfield went to Buckingham Junior High. Some of the kids that went to that school were nice and some were bad. A lot of the guys used to have little singing groups and they would sing doo-wop songs in the hallways after school. They sounded real good. I wished I could sing like that; maybe then I could get a girlfriend. I used to envy the other guys. Every day after school they would walk their girlfriends home, carrying their books and singing to them.

I was still struggling with my math, and, of course, Deacon Dockett never took the time to sit down with me and help me with my homework, probably because he didn't know how to do math himself. He had a third-grade education and couldn't read. I guess he didn't want me to wind up like him and that's why he would get so upset when I got bad marks on my report card. He would intimidate me and scare me half to death, threatening to beat the crap out of me if I didn't improve my schoolwork.

The clothes that the Docketts had me wearing in school made me a laughing-stock among the other kids. I wore high-water pants with worn-out sneakers with holes in the bottoms, and shirts that were too small; the sleeves had holes in the elbows and were tight on my skinny arms. The Dockett made me wear my hair in a crew cut. I used to see the girls walking down the hallway pointing at me and laughing. I was so ashamed of the clothes that Deacon Dockett made me wear to school. In the school gym when we changed into our gym clothes, I would hide behind a locker so no one would see my holey socks. Each day when school let out I had to just about run home because I had to be home at a certain time or catch hell from the deacon. So while the other kids were walking with their friends and carrying their girl's books, I looked like the Roadrunner dashing down the street in my raggedy sneakers and high-water pants. God forbid I be late getting home!

Chapter 22

My "Family"

Sundays most of my time was spent in church. I had to be in Sunday school in the morning and then stay for morning services. After the morning services we would go home and Mrs. Dockett would cook a big Southern-style meal. She was a good cook; I just hoped that I could enjoy the meal without getting hit at the table.

After dinner we would head back to church for evening services, with Deacon Dockett saying amen all day and Mrs. Dockett rocking back and forth in her pew, fanning herself saying, "Amen, amen." Sundays my wardrobe was a little better, although the white shirts that I had to wear were tight-fitting around my neck and my necktie felt like a noose. My suit was a little too small; it was tight-fitting and the pants were high-water. My shoes weren't too bad, kind of old-fashioned but I learned to live with them. In all actuality I looked like a church "nerd." The choir robe that I wore covered up the clothes anyway. While standing in the choir, I would occasionally glance over at Deacon Dockett. I would catch him rolling his eyes at me as if to say, "I'm watching you, mister, you better not blink or scratch or cough or sneeze or breath, period!" That's the look that Deacon Dockett gave me in church. I looked forward to going to church. I knew that Emma and Sandy would be there, and just the sight of them helped ease my agony. I was in love!

It was a hot summer day, and as usual I was out in the garden pulling weeds. Mr. Dockett came to the door and called me inside. *Now what did I do?* Maybe I wasn't pulling the weeds from his garden fast enough. I couldn't figure out what it was that I did but I was preparing myself for another butt whipping in any case.

When I got in the house he said, "There is someone here to see you." There was dirt and grime all over my clothes and he wanted me to see somebody? He told me to go into the living room and when I did I saw a young-looking colored man sitting on the couch. He was dressed real sharp. We shook hands and he introduced himself to me. He said his name was Charles O'Neil and that he was my older brother! Well, needless to say, I was speechless. I thought that I only had three brothers, Arnold, Michael, and Tony. He went on to explain to me how he found me and that he was going to try to get me out of this foster home. I asked him some more questions about himself. He said that after he was born the state placed him in an orphanage until he turned seventeen years old. When he got out he moved to Boston, Massachusetts, and settled down. He then started searching for his family.

He said that he found out that our brother Arnold was in a state school, and when he went to visit him Arnold told him about the beatings that he was getting at the school every day. He said that Arnold told him that if he ever had the chance he would run away from that school. Charles said that he found me when he called the D.C.G. They told him where I was living. And then while walking down the street in Springfield one day looking for me, he happened to stop an older woman and ask her if she knew a kid named Alex O'Neil. He said she gave him a strange look and said yes, why? Charles told her that he was my brother and that he was looking for me. As fate would have it, the woman that he spoke with happened to be my aunt Dorothy Domino. What a coincidence!

He went on to say that she took him to her house on Stebbins Street, which was just around the corner from where I was living, and introduced him to more members of the family. He told me that "Aunt Dot" explained to him what had happened to our mother. She told him that after he was born he was placed in an orphanage, and a few years later our mom was incarcerated in a woman's state farm in Connecticut. At that time she was pregnant with Arnold and me. At the time of our birth she was taken out of the farm and placed in a hospital in a small town in Connecticut. After we were born, both Arnold and myself were immediately placed in the D.C.G. This was about 1944. In December of the same year, our mother was placed in the Belchertown State School in Belchertown, Massachusetts. She passed away on April 7, 1949, from pulmonary tuberculosis. She was twenty-seven years old. Arnold and I were five years old at the time of her death. We never had the opportunity to meet her.

Stebbins Street was only a block away from where I lived, and he was telling me that I had a lot of relatives right around the corner from there! I couldn't help but wonder why I was never told about them. I wonder if Aunt Dot or anybody in my family knew about me or my whereabouts. After listening to my brother Charles, I couldn't help but wonder if somebody was hiding something from me. How could you live in the same neighborhood with relatives and not know it?

Anyway, Charles said that he talked with the state people and maybe they could get me out of this foster home and have me placed with my relatives. He also said that one day he would take me over to meet my relatives. We talked for a little longer, getting acquainted with each other, and then he said, "Well, brother, I've got to be getting back to Boston. But I will be back to see you again real soon." I didn't want to see him go but at least I knew that he would try to get me out of the Docketts' home.

I guess Mr. Dockett eavesdropped on the conversation, because as soon as my brother Charles left he stood in front of me with a real mean look on his face and pointed his finger in my face, saying, "I better not ever catch you over to those people's house, you hear me?" I guess he felt that they would be a bad influence on me. He said that if he ever caught me over there I would be sorry. Here I was, fifteen years old, spent all of my childhood life in foster homes; now I finally found my relatives and I couldn't see them!

Well, needless to say, after a few weeks of anguish I couldn't resist going over to see my relatives. So one day after school, I ran faster than I usually do just to buy myself some time. I went over to the address on Stebbins Street that Charles gave me. As I got closer a strange feeling came over me. I didn't know what I would say when I got there. I was experiencing mixed emotions. The big question in my mind was would they accept me. The question was why wasn't there an attempt to get me out of the foster homes?

When I reached the house I said to myself, "Well, here goes." It was a two-family house with a wide front porch and a small front yard that desperately needed grass. I knocked and waited a few minutes. A young, light-skinned girl came to the door and asked me what I wanted. I told her who I was and the next thing I knew I was in the house surrounded by a half-dozen people introducing themselves to me: cousins, aunts, uncles, nephews. My Aunt Dot lived on the first floor and my grandmother Annie Robbins and Grandfather "Flossy" lived on the second floor, along with my two uncles, Tony and Andrew. What a feeling—my real family! I only wish that Arnold was there to meet them.

My Aunt Dot said that my brother Charles told them all about me. It was a great feeling. Everybody was friendly towards me, hugging me and shaking my hand. I could see the tears in my grandmother's eyes when my Aunt Dot introduced me to her. My grandmother told me that my father lived downtown and that they never heard from him. I was so caught up in the excitement that I forgot all about my curfew. I was supposed to be home a half hour ago! Before I left, Aunt Dot told me that she and my brother Charles discussed plans to have me taken out of the foster home and placed with them. She said that they met with my social worker Mr. Gibbons, and plans were being made. I was ecstatic. I was on cloud nine. Pretty soon this would be my new home with my real relatives. No more beatings, no more weed pulling, no more punishments for little or nothing.

When I got out outside I started running down the street in order to make up some of the time that I used up at my *family*'s home. I was scared now. I knew that I was in a world of trouble. I just hoped that Mr. Dockett was not home when I got there. As I dashed down the street I spotted a familiar car parked at the end of the street, and my heart sank. Parked down at the end of the street was Deacon Dockett. I guess he wasn't home.

There was no doubt in my mind that Deacon Percival Dockett saw me coming out of my family's house. I guess he figured out that since I was not home on time I had to be at my relatives' house. I didn't even know that he knew where they lived. I know now, though! I prayed that when I got home my execution would be swift and painless. Mr. Dockett drove off and was waiting for me when I got home.

When I arrived home, Mr. Dockett seemed calm at first. I thought to myself, *Oh, maybe it won't be so bad after all.* Boy was I wrong! Without a word, Deacon Dockett came up to me and slapped me in the face and screamed at me, "Didn't I tell you not to go over to *them people*'s house, didn't I? But no, you got to be hard headed." He slapped me again then picked up a shoe and started beating me with it, saying, "Someday you will learn that a hard head gets you a soft behind." Mrs.

Dockett tried to stop him from beating on me but he wouldn't listen to her. He kept it up, causing me to fall down the stairs, with him right behind me still flailing away on me. After what seemed like an eternity he finally stopped and said, "Now go to your room." I ran back upstairs with tears in my eyes. I slammed my door shut and flopped down on my bed and cried like a baby. I hated these people.

Another day while I was "hanging out" in the backyard digging up weeds, I saw this light-skinned guy wearing a uniform come into the yard. As he got closer I recognized him. It was my brother Tony, "the bossy cow." He looked good in his Marine Corps uniform. I knew right then and there that that was what I was going to do when I got older. I was going to be a United States Marine like John Wayne and Tony. We shook hands. He asked me, "How were things going?" I told him that I met my real brother Charles and all my relatives, and that they were going to get me out of there. He said that he was glad to hear that, and he hoped that things would work out for me. He said that he went over to see Michael and that's how he found out where I was. He said that he didn't like the Marines because they made him do things that he didn't like to do and that he was going to get out soon. We talked a little longer, then Tony said, "Well, man, I got to be going. I've got places to go, and things to do before I go back to base." We shook hands and he turned and left. He still had that cocky attitude and walked with that swagger. I hated to see him go. He turned and waved at me saying, "Hang in there."

During the time that we were talking, I occasionally glanced at the house to see if Deacon Dockett would come outside to see who it was that I was talking to. I saw him looking out of the window. I guess he thought that Tony was a recruiter and maybe he was trying to recruit me. He never asked me who it was and I never told him.

Every now and them my brother Michael would ride his bike over to visit me. I asked him how the people that he was staying with were. He said that they were nice. "A little strict but nice." At least he could go out and ride his bike and be with the other kids in his neighborhood. I asked him if he had seen Tony. He said, "Yeah, man, and I liked his uniform too." Our minds were made up. As soon as we got old enough we were going to enlist in the Marines.

I was still getting bad report cards in school. I hated math. I wanted to quit school and go into the service like my brother Tony did. I knew that Deacon Percival Dockett wasn't about to hear that. "Hell no!"

I spent a lot of time in my room on punishment for one thing or another. I took advantage of that time by reading. I used to love reading detective magazines that I "bought" in the store and smuggled into my room. My favorite was a series by Richard S. Prather, mystery novels about a private detective named Shell Scott. I was obsessed with those novels. I would read them over and over, especially when I was under punishment. I wanted to be a private detective some day and catch bad guys single-handed like Shell Scott.

Every now and then Mr. Gibbons would come by and visit me. He would ask me how things were going. I wanted so much to tell him about the constant beatings that I was getting and the "milk thing" that happened. There was so much that I wanted to tell him, but I was too afraid because I felt that Mr. Dockett would beat me when Mr. Gibbons left. And I was tired of the beatings. So I lied and said that everything was all right. I asked him if he had heard from my brother Charles and my aunt Dorothy Domino. He said yes but he couldn't make any promises yet.

Charles and Mr. Gibbons met and arrangements were made to have me removed from the Docketts and placed with my grandparents on Stebbins Street. There was still some red tape that had to be passed before the move was made, but at least I had something to look forward to. It was a strange feeling knowing that I was leaving the Docketts to live with my relatives but a good feeling as well. I just wished that day would come. Deacon Dockett didn't beat me as much as he did before. I guess he figured that it wasn't worth it since I was leaving. Mrs. Dockett said that she was sorry to see me leave but it was in my best interest because Deacon Dockett was fed up with me and she didn't want to see me get hurt by him.

It was late one summer evening and I was out in the backyard doing my chores. Deacon Dockett called me into the house, and upon entering the house I saw my state man Mr. Gibbons and my brother Charles sitting at the kitchen table. Mrs. Dockett was signing some papers that Mr. Gibbons had brought with him. I sat down and Charles said that I would be moving to my grandmother's house this Saturday. After the papers were signed Charles and Mr. Gibbons told me they would see me on Saturday. They then left. I was very excited and speechless.

The day that I'd been waiting for finally came. Early Saturday morning, Mr. Gibbons arrived. He asked me if I was ready to go and of course I said, "Yes, sir." I thought to myself, *If you only knew.*

After saying our goodbyes, we left the Docketts for good. Upon our arrival at my grandparents' home, we were greeted by my aunt Dot. She showed me to my room and asked me if I was hungry. That was strange; no one has ever asked me if I was hungry! I said no thank you. I already knew most of the people that were there. I had met them all when I was sneaking over to see them. Mr. Gibbons talked with my grandmother briefly, telling her that he would be coming around from time to time to check up on me and that if she needed anything to call him. He said that I should be happy here and he would be back in a couple of weeks to see how I adjusted to my new home. With that he left.

After the hugs and handshakes, I went up to my room and sat down on the bed. My thoughts drifted to my brother Arnold. I wished they could have gotten him out of Belchertown School. What a wonderful feeling. No more beatings or getting yelled at. I could eat whenever I wanted to. I could go anywhere I wanted to, when I wanted to. I could even watch television if I wanted to. Those were luxuries that I never had. There was a vast amount of freedom that I now had. I felt like I was in another world. What a strange feeling.

For a while I was sort of apprehensive about going into the refrigerator for fear of being scolded. When I entered the living room, I expected to get yelled at and told to get out! I could even go into the den and watch TV and not get beaten. It was a strange feeling and I knew it would take time for me to adjust to this vast amount of freedom. I spent a lot of time talking with my grandmother about my past. She tried to explain to me the things that happened to my mom and why they couldn't get me to live with them back then.

I spent a lot of time with my grandfather too. He wasn't my biological grandfather but he was a gentleman. He treated me like his own grandson, and I loved him for that. He used to ask me to go with him to the package store around the corner to play his number, which was 6363, and he would always buy one "nip" of brandy. This was a daily ritual with him. He was a hard-working man. He was a rubbish collector for the city. I was proud of him. He kept food on the table and in my stomach, and that was something my stomach was not used to yet! When my brother Michael found out where I was, he came over to see me. He was happy for me. He said it wasn't bad where he was either; his foster parents were firm but not mean. And they didn't beat on him. He said that he was going into the service next year, probably the Marines.

Mike in the Marines 1963-1967

Chapter 23

"Free At Last"

Life with my grandparents was great. I started hanging out on the weekends with my cousins, going to house parties, block dances, and high school dances, even bars. I didn't know how to dance nor did I know how to talk to girls, but I had fun anyway.

I was what they used to call "lame," meaning "square," "a nerd," "not with it." There was one girl that I went out with. That relationship lasted a whole week! Her name was Loretha. I was in love. She had a nice shape and was pretty. I wanted to marry her and live happily ever after. She was nice to me but I guess I wasn't her type. I couldn't take her to high school dances. I didn't have a car, and when I did get the opportunity to go to a dance I couldn't dance worth a damn. I didn't know how to "rap" with her. Kissing her was a disaster; my lips kept missing hers. She would start laughing at me then I would get mad and walk away.

I remember one evening when I was visiting her at her house. I guess her father decided to stay home that evening. We were sitting on the couch in the front room, her on one end and me on the other. Her dad decided to join us. He sat in an armchair across from us and picked up a newspaper and pretended to be reading it. I think he had a peephole in it and was watching me through it to make sure that I was being a gentleman. It was a very uncomfortable situation. I didn't know what to say to her in front of him, and she didn't have too much to say me. We just sat there watching TV like two lame ducks.

Finally, I couldn't take it anymore, so I told her that I had to be going. I said goodbye to her father. He kind of reminded me of Deacon Dockett; he even looked like him. He was light-complexioned and wore thick, horned-rimmed glasses. He was slightly bald. Who knows, maybe he and the Deacon were related. Maybe Deacon Dockett called him and told him to watch out for me because I was a bad guy or something. Who knows?

Anyway, when Loretha walked me to the door I gave her a sloppy kiss somewhere on her cheek and said, "Goodnight, I will see you in school tomorrow," and left. It ended up being a very short relationship. Eventually she decided to let me go. I guess her friends told her that "she could do better than that." So she "dumped" me.

That was that.

I started drinking and hanging out in the street almost every day. My relatives did as much as they could for me. I wanted new clothes and they couldn't afford to get them for me, so I took on some small jobs. Jobs like picking tobacco in the tobacco fields every summer. I used to shine shoes in a smoke shop in downtown Springfield, and I worked as a stock boy in a department store called Forbes and Wallace in downtown Springfield. My job was to fold sweaters and shirts and place them in a stock room. It wasn't a bad job. Every now and then I would go to school wearing a *new* sweater or shirt. There was a department store called Kings in Winchester Square in Springfield. I used to work with a janitorial service there. I remember that they had a nice line of shoes. But for some strange reason, one of the boxes of shoes would always end up with a pair of old shoes in it. I don't know how that happened.

Once every month Aunt Dot would take me to the welfare place to pick up welfare cheese, powdered milk, cereal, and anything else she could get her hands on. There was definitely "no shame in her game" at all. Aunt Dot was one of a kind. I remember she used to take me to the Goodwill stores to get me some school clothes. I hated it when she had whoever was driving go right down Main Street to the Goodwill store, where everybody could see me. I used to be so embarrassed, especially if I saw somebody that I knew. I used to duck down in the seat of the car when somebody that I knew passed by. Aunt Dot was only doing what she thought was right. She was trying to take care of me the best that she could. God bless her.

There was this girl named Gail that lived one street over from me, and all of the kids used to hang out at her house every night, even on the weekdays. Her mom was cool, but her father was a little different.

He used to hate to see us come over. We used to listen to records, play cards, and some of the guys smoked "reefer" and drank cheap wine. I met this cool kid name Ronnie Hurst. We used to hang out. Ronnie was "hip"—that was the slang for being cool back then. I liked hanging with Ronnie; he was crazy. We had a lot of fun drinking beer, chasing girls, and playing baseball at the welfare park on Oak Grove Avenue. He tried to teach me to be "hip" like him but I was a hard case. He gave up on me but we still hung out together.

I remember one day we had just finished playing baseball and Ronnie said, "Let's go get a soda, man, I'm thirsty as hell." So Ronnie and another kid named Ricky Fredricks and me stopped in a store called Pete's and bought two Coca-Colas. Ricky and Ronnie used to always argue with each other about trivial things. Ricky told Ronnie not to throw his empty soda bottle up against the wall, but he did anyway, shattering the bottle, sending a large piece of glass into my face.

At first I thought that it just hit me and bounced off, but suddenly I felt warm blood flowing down my face onto my shirt. I put my tongue where the glass hit and there was a huge hole in my jaw. I poked my tongue through it and you could see my tongue protruding out of the side of my face. I ripped off my shirt and wrapped it around my face to stop the bleeding. Ronnie looked at me and kept saying he was sorry and that he didn't mean to do that. I knew that he didn't mean it. I wasn't mad at him. Ricky said, "See, man? I told you not to throw that bottle against the wall, now look what you did." Ricky helped me pack my shirt against my jaw to stop the bleeding and we all walked to the

Wesson Hospital on State Street. Luckily it wasn't too far from where we were.

When we arrived at the hospital I was quickly rushed into a room with doctors and nurses. Somebody called the police. When they came they kept asking me who "cut" me. I told them nobody cut me. I tried to explain to them that it was an accident but they didn't believe me and kept demanding that I tell them who cut me. Finally, after realizing that I may be telling the truth, they left.

As time went on I kind of lost track of Ronnie. I found out later when I returned from Vietnam that Ronnie Hurst had joined the Army and was killed in Vietnam. The only thing that I have to remember Ronnie by is the scar on my face.

My junior high school years were spent at Buckingham Junior high and I went to Trade high school in my senior years. I felt that I didn't need school and no one forced me to go, and I knew that if I quit no one was going to beat on me. I hated school anyway, so I quit.

As time went on I could see myself going downhill, hanging out, partying day in and day out. One day while I was hanging with the guys, I ran into my friend Bernard, the same person that gave me the Tang at the Docketts. He asked me how I was doing and what was I doing for myself. I said, "Nothing right now." He asked me if I had any plans for my future. I told him that I had quit school and was looking for another job. He said that I was making a terrible mistake and that I was heading down the wrong road. He said that at some point I would have to make a decision about what I was going to do with my life. Bernard told me that there were two roads to take in life. One was the bad road that will take you nowhere except downhill. And then there is the right road that will take you far in life. The question is which road are you going to take?

Later that evening, when I found my way home after "hanging" in the street, I sat in my room and thought about what Bernard had said. I knew that he was right. I could see that I was on the "wrong road," and I could see where I was heading. At that point I made my decision. I was eighteen years old. In September of 1963 I enlisted in the Marine Corps.

My childhood was over.

"Someday I'll wish upon a star, and wake up where the clouds are far behind me."

"Me in the Marines"

The Massachusetts Department of Social Services (D.S.S.) copies of original documentation of social workers' visits to each of the foster homes of the "four boys" from 1948 to 1961.

(Courtesy of the Massachusetts Department of Social Services Archives, Boston, Massachusetts)

NOTE: EACH FILE IS A COMPLETE PAGE scanned at 300 dpi

Arnold Barry O'Neil

32052 - C

O'NEILL, Arnold (P)

(Wi. Mrs.   n, Richmond)

11/18/52 - (J.H.Melville) Visitor called at the Richmond Grade School and talked with the principal and boy's teacher. Boy appears to be doing average work in school. Stated that the smaller one of the twins, Alexander, is the smarter and better behaved. Neither are over-bright, but are presenting no specific problem in the home. The bigger boy, Arnold, is a small behavior problem but the principal and the teacher did not feel that they presented any problem to the school or community at this time. The principal is not overly enthusiastic in talking about the boys; he seems to be rather disinterested in them.   (RSS)

11/26/52 - (J.H.Melville) Mrs.   , foster mother, in to the office on 11/26/52 to talk to visitor. Visitor had called on two previous occasions and unable to find her at home. Mrs.   an revealed that her husband is to be released in the near future and she was interested in any information that we could give her concerning the possible removal of the children, if her husband was returned. She is prepared for their removal. She would like time enough to prepare the children and it was agreed that as soon as this Department made up its mind concerning removal, she would be notified and at the same time she would be in touch with visitor about the possible return of her husband.   (RSS)

12/29/52 - (J.H.Melville) Placed with Mrs.   , Cole Avenue, Pittsfield. (P). B&C. Reason: Family's moral condition.   (RSS)

*12/12/52 - (J.H.Melville) Visitor to home of Mrs.   Richmond and talked with foster mother. Revealed to her that we were successful in obtaining a new foster home for the children now placed in her home, and were making arrangements for removal of the four children now under her care. Foster mother was very much upset by the news, but stated at the same time that she is very much relieved as she has been under a strain wondering when the children were to be removed. She stated she felt it would have been much kinder if the children had been removed at the time her husband had got into his difficulties, which had cause him to be removed to jail, but realized that at the time it had been felt that the removal of the children on top of all her other troubles would have been a severe blow to her. Mrs.   inquired as to who the new family was to be. Stated she knew Mr. and Mrs.   in Pittsfield by reputation, but not personally. She is to keep the children until after Christmas, at which time they will be removed. When first notified Mrs.   stated she did not want to keep the children for Christmas, but later agreed that it would be more difficult for the children i they were removed before Christmas. Foster mother was very emotional and it is obvious that it is going to be a very upsetting experience when the actual separation takes place. During the course of conversation the children came in from school and foster mother, who had pre-viously prepared them for leaving, broke the news to them that they were to have a new home after Christmas. Both of the O'Neill twins started to cry, although Anthony Gregory said noth-ing. Mrs.   was crying as she told them the news, and visitor talked to the children for a short time, but obviously they did not understand fully the change which will take place. Following this, visitor talked with foster mother for some time, discussed the necesary mech-anics of moving and told her that he would give her plenty of notice so that she might have all the children's clothing prepared. She agreed that she would continue to prepare the chil-dren for moving. Visitor decided that it would be best not to prolong the in erview as both Mrs.   and the children were very upset by the news.   (AJS)

*12/16/52 - (J.H.Melville) Visitor to   Home, Cole Avenue. It was agreed that children would be removed from .   ome 12/29/53 to .   Home. Mrs.   appeared grateful that children would have a week in the home to become adjusted before it would be necessary to re-turn to school. Visitor will inform Mrs.   that children are to be removed on 12/29/52.   (AJS)

32053-C   -10-

O'NEILL, ARNOLD   (P)

(Wi. Mrs.   , Cole Avenue, Pittsfield) B&C

5/6/53 (continued) get nothing from another year in her class. Visitor had
the impression also that she was not particularly looking forward to another
year with the boy. She is rather an odd, excitable person, and perhaps with
another teacher, the boy may be better controlled. Visitor feels that this
boy should be tested at Belchertown in the near future.   (js)

7/7/53 - (J.Melville) Visitor to   home, talked to O'Neill twins and
foster mother. Talked with boys alone and in the presence of foster mother.
In the presence of foster mother, boys say very little, even when visitor
was talking to them some distance from the house out in the area where the
family has their chickens. Boys appeared scared of their foster mother.
They cast glances in her direction before talking. They were unwilling to
say anything which might reflect upon her. Their chief news seemed to be
that they had seen their former foster mother, Mrs.   at a mutual
friend's home a few days before. They said that they were very glad to see
her and they hoped that she would come and see them at the   home, but
they were not too hopeful of this. They said that they were well-treated
and usually got enough to eat, especially when Mr.   fed them. They
said that they liked it in the home and were allowed to play as much as they
wanted to. Behind all this, one felt that these boys were not telling the
whole story. Their glances toward the house, or toward Mrs.   when she
was in the yard were not those of boys who seem to really enjoy the home as
much as they said. Perhaps, Visitor is reading into the boy's attitude, but
it does seem that they were not as happy as they were in the   . home,
which is the only comparison worker can make, not having known them before
that time. Boys were examined at the home by Dr.   who just happened
to be making a call on the   ' granddaughter, who has the measles. He was
somewhat taken back by their thinness, but again, this might be explained by
the fact that boys are growing taller, and using their energy in that way,
rather than in filling out. Worker did try to stress with Mrs.   that he
was not happy with the boys physical condition and their attitude, and that
some improvement would have to be shown by Mrs.   in their care if they
were to remain there.   (js)

7/24/53 - (J.Melville) Worker to   home, talked with foster mother about
the possibility of the children placed in her home going to summer camp. At
this time the Worker had in mind the   camp located in Williamstown. Work
er had checked with the Boys Club and found that at the present time they did
not have any openings, but they had promised to call if it were possible for
the children to go there this summer. Mrs.   stated that she thought two
weeks or more at camp would be very beneficial for the boys. Worker had thou
thought there would be a little hostility to the idea and was surprised by he
attitude, although she stated that she did not feel that Tony   would
benefit from it. She felt that he was a bad influence upon the boys and wondered if it were not possible to send the other three children one week, and
if Tony had to go at all, let him go by himself. She feels that Tony is behind most of the trouble she is having with the children. She feels quite
strongly about it, and even asked that Tony be removed from her home. All
four boys came in from playing while Worker was there and Worker had a chance
to talk with them for a short time. All were in need of haircuts. Mrs.
manner of speaking to the boys is pretty harsh at times. They seem to fear h
                                                                 (js)

155

32052-C

O'NEILL, Arnold

(W1. Mrs. '   .   ,   , Cole Avenue, Pittsfield) B & C

7/24/53 (continued) Worker to Williamstown, talked with Mrs.   who operates the summer camp regarding the children who we plan to send to camp here.
It was agreed that the children will be sent within the next two weeks. Final
date would be agreed upon later.   (js)

8/1/53 - (J.Melville) Worker received a call the previous night from Mr.
at the Boys Club in Pittsfield, who stated that they would have room for the
four colored children, Tony Gregory, Alex and Arnold O'Neill and Gary
for the next two weeks at Camp Russell Richmond and he wondered if boys could
be ready to go to camp on very short notice, namely one day. He wanted them
to go to Camp August 1-15. Worker felt that in spite of the other arrangements
which had been made to send boys to camp in Williamstown, this was a better
opportunity. They would be at a camp where there were much better physical
resources, it would be a mixed group and not a strictly colored group, and
Worker felt that it would be good for the boys to work into this type of a
group if at all possible, inasmuch as their school work and after-hour play
they are continually with white children. Worker called and made arrangements
with Mrs.   and boys went to camp this date.   (js)

8/1/53 - (J.Melville) PLACED WITH CAMP RUSSELL RICHMOND. APPROVED BY EJM.
#72 to summer camp.   (js)

8/3/53 - (J.Melville) Received a call from Mr.   and later went to Boys
Club to talk with him regarding the four children. It seems that for the
present time it was necessary for the children to sleep at the Central Build-
ing because they did not have the necessary blankets or warm clothing to allow them to remain in the camp overnight. Worker was successful in obtaining
necessary blankets from the Board of Public Welfare at the City Infirmary.
Worker delivered these to Mr.   who took them to the camp.   (js)

8/4/53 - (J.Melville) Worker to Grant's, Inc., Pittsfield, did shopping for
children at Camp. They went to camp very hurriedly and foster mother was not
able to have all the necessary items.   (js)

8/11/53 - (J.Melville) Worker to Camp Russell to see the boys. Unfortunately
all four of the boys were on a hike this day and Worker did not see them.
Talked with Mr. Fahey who was leaving when Worker arrived. He stated that
boys were getting along extremely well, had tremendous appetites and seemed
to mix fairly well with the rest of the boys in the camp. He said that they
had told him how much they were enjoying it and he knew that it was going to
be difficult for them to get used to the idea of going home in a few days. (j)

8/15/53 - (J.Melville) PLACED WITH MRS.   ,   Cole Avenue,
Pittsfield. #79 return from from Camp.
Approved by EJM.   (js)

8/17/53 - (J.Melville) Worker to   home, boys were now home from camp
and were playing in the back yard. All four of them enjoyed the camp trem-
endously. Worker learned from foster mother and from boys that Tony
had been crying very hard when he returned from camp and stated that he would
run away if he were not allowed to go back. He seemed quite upset even today
which was after he was home for 3 or 4 days. All the boys asked if they could
return next year for a longer period. They spoke of the fine meals they had
there and how they had gone back for 2nds and 3rds at every meal. Two or three
of the boys had left clothing at the Boys Club and Worker took them down and

32052-C

O'NEILL, Arnold

(w1. Mrs.   -   5 Cole Avenue, Pittsfield B&C

Arnold claims that Anthony Gregory said that any time he has money,
Anthony makes him share it or takes it all, always goes through his pockets
at night. Worker impressed upon him the seriousness of the problem.
Foster mother has been informed, seemed to be genuinely concerned about
the problem, said that she knew of Anthony's taking from Arnold and had
punished him for this.   (bac)

1/20/54 - (J.MElville) Worker to home. Talked with foster mother. This boy is her favorite
of the four placed in the home and difficult perhaps to see why. He definitely causes her
more trouble than any of the other boys, is a very active youngster who in many ways does not
know right from wrong as shown by his actions in his school, stealing from teachers and pupils
etc. Foster mother's opinion isthat Arnold is brighter than the other children. Is not borne
out by recent test at Belchertown State School where he made one of the poorer marks. She
believes that the reason for his poor school work is that Arnold likes attention and tries to
obtain this attention by doing poor work and is then singled out by the teacher for attention
even though it is a poor type of attention. He doesn't appear to know the difference. Stated
that she is able to punish him successfully by taking away privileges, keepinghim in the house
after school if he does not behave himself and this seems to break him of many of his bad habits
Worker had obtained a bicycle, asked foster mother if she would want this for the children. She
stated that she did not at the present time, did not feel the children were responsible enough
to own a bike. Stated that she preferred to keep them in the immediate area of the home. This
has been her attitude all along regarding the children. Worker does not believe that they have
too much freedom. Recently,however, they have begun to seea few movies, etc. something that
they did not do in the past. Children all attend church regularly at the present time. (LG)

2/19/54 - (J.Melville) Worker to Redfield School and talked with Arnold's teacher and principal. Also saw some prime examples of Arnold's work which is terrible. He either does everything all wrong or he writes it so illegibly that you cannot tell whether it is right or
wrong. The rest of the class is being disturbed by him. Principal stated that his teacher
was his first year teacher. She was unable to teach boy, was much to lenient with the boy all
year long. Worker had talked with her about a special class which had been recommended in the
Belchertown examination and Miss Berte said that she now felt it would be best if boy could be
placed in this special class. She said that she would look into the matter and if worker would
call within a few weeks she would let him know what decision she had reached.   (LG)

3/19/54 - (J. Melville) Annual physical examination by Dr.
Pittsfield. Height: 56 in., Weight: 61 lbs. Development: thin normal
child. Recommendations: none.   (ES)

2/12/54 - (J. Melville) Worker to home, left some clothing for Alex and
Arnold which had been given to Worker by another foster mother. Clothing
was in very good repair and it worked out very nicely with the O'Neil twins.
Foster mother had been somewhat difficult regarding clothing. She does not
spend anywhere near the boys' normal allowance, as a result the children
are poorly clothed and do not make their best appearance. Foster mother
appears to be very fond of Arnold, stated she did not receive any more poor
reports from school on the two children. She was somewhat disturbed by the
manners of both children, said that Alex in particular had some very bad
habits when outside the home. Had observed him on several occasions going
into neighbors' yards and taking things from their garbage pails. Worker
questioned whether the boy is really getting enough to eat in this home. She

32052-C

O'NEILL, Arnold

(W1. Mrs.   ˙ Cole Avenue, Pittsfield) B&C

<u>2/12/54 - (J. Melville)</u> (cont.) assured Worker that boy was, could not under-
stand the reason for his actions. She is somewhat disappointed in the children
(ES)

<u>3/18/54 - (J. Melville)</u> Worker to Redfield School and talked with boy's
teacher and principal. Miss   the Principal, feels that perhaps Arnold
would be helped by being placed in the special class recently organized in
Pittsfield. Lately his work in the third grade has become much too difficult
for him and as a result of this he has become more of a behavior problem in
class inasmuch as he has so much time on his hands. The problem regarding
the special class is one of transportation. The school would be some distance
from the home and it would be necessary for the boy to go by bus. Miss I __
said that she would refer the boy to the Guidance Director and if they deemed
it advisable perhaps a transfer would be made.

<u>3/22/54 - (J. Melville)</u> Worker to Mercer School where the special class
for retarded children is conducted. Talked with Mrs.   ' the special
class teacher and also with Mrs.   _ who is in charge of retarded program.
There are approximately one dozen children in this class, but it would appear
that they have a considerable lower I. Q. than Arnold and after observing
the children in class for sometime and talking with the people in charge of
the program it was decided that Arnold perhaps would benefit by being with
normal children rather than trying to be placed with children who have even
less ability than himself. Worker later made a call at Redfield School and
explained views regarding this decision to the Principal who agreed with the
findings and who felt that another year might make a difference in Arnold.
She hoped that with a new teacher who perhaps would be more firm and more'
experienced, boy could progress more satisfactory.   (ES

<u>3/26/54 - (J. Melville)</u> Worker to the home and talked with foster mother
and with Arnold who evidently has been saving his papers for a considerable
period of time and they are all marked A or B, although a quick glance at
some of the papers show that the mark given was probably given for encourage-
ment only as the work was very substandard. Alex appears to be doing slightly
better than Arnold. During visits to the school, teacher seems to be more
concerned about Arnold than his brother.

Worker has been somewhat disturbed by continuing difficulty with this home.
~~There are so many poor points to be found that continued use of this home~~
seems rather futile. Foster mother is very uncooperative, refuses to accept
supervision and if pressed about matters of policies becomes very argumentative
and difficult. It took almost one year and one-half of constant prodding
before she would take four children for an annual physical. Worker has never
been able to get her to provide the children with milk at a noon day meal
which they have at school. The lunches which the children take vary between
bearly adequate and insufficient. During recent physical examination all
four children needed vitamins and treatment for one condition or another.
Worker discussed these things with her today, but Worker got the impression
it would be another struggle to get foster mother to carry out the various
requests. The home is being used because of a lack of another colored foster
home facility. If she were willing to cooperate this could be an excellent
home because the physical appearances are exceptional. Worker believes that
the situation will get worse when Mrs.   two boys come home from the

32052-C   -18-

O'NEILL, Arnold

(With Mrs. ⁞   -- ⁞   ⁞ole Avenue, Pittsfield)B&C

8/31/54 had sent them to bed as punishment several times without their meals, but that was only
done in the beginning and not of late.

Anthony, she said, has bus tickets which she allows him to use as he sees fit. However, he
occasionally walks to school with several of his friends and sells the tickets to buy ice cream
or candy. I asked her if Anthony took his lunch from the house and she said that he does this,
but then I questioned her about his milk which most of the children buy at school. She said
she is not able to give him money for a beverage because it is too expensive and if she did give
him money, she is sure that it would be spent on candy rather than on milk. The other children,
she said, have been coming home for lunch during the school lunch time although they did occasio
ally eat at school.

In the afternoons the boys come home immediately after school. I asked her if they played with
any of the boys in the neighborhood. She said she does not want them hanging around anywhere el
because she is afraid that they will be very easily led and that squabbles or difficulties will
be blamed on these boys rather than on any other neighborhood boys. She said that the yard is
large enough for them to play here and they can participate in baseball and football games right
in the yard. In addition, she said, there are swings and other playthings. In addition, she sa
there are swings and other playthings.

This summer she and Anthony worked in the vegetable garden. The boys have an enormous appetite
and she states that the food bill is over $50 a week. When they first came, in addition to eati
their regular meals, they would rummage through the neighborhood asking for food from neighbors
or eating from garbage cans, but she said that this has not occurred lately except for one incident that happened last week. The family had finished dinner and the boys went out into the
garden and ate almost all of the tomatoes from their garden. She sees no reason for this other
than the fact that they were greedy and does not directly relate it at all to the fact that they
might have been hungry. She said that the boys know that they can always have a second helping
and that particular evening they stated that they had ample food.

I asked her why the boys don't play with the other youngsters in the neighborhood as it is actua
ly within walking distance of their own home and she quickly said that there are no boys of
Anthony's age here. This is a direct falsehood as Worker knows that there are two boys his age
who live almost next door. Later in the conversation she mentioned these two boys and reversed
her former statement, but said that these youngsters are working all summer and that there is no
one here for Anythony to be with. Worker spoke to her about all the other complaints that I had
received, but she had an answer ready as denial for every one of them.

When the boys came here, she said that they were not able to do anything for themselves and she
felt that their training had been extremely poor and she had to start anew as if they were babie
Even after two years of Anthony's placement, he does not come in to use the bathroom, but rather
soils his pants although she said that the house is never locked and he is certainly free to com
in whenever it is necessary. This, and the subsequent behavior of Anthony, is probably relate
directly to his dislike for Mrs. Evans and his actions as retaliation and feeling toward her.
Anthony is the boy who actually told the neighbors/that they received here in the home. She wer
on to say that the boys did not even know how to dress themselves. Her teachings were long an
arduous and even now, they will not do anything unless they are specifically told what to do and
someone is telling them.

This summer, she said, has been comparatively good. The main difficulty with the children occu
during the school year. She feels that they are all slow mentally, although Gary(Michael) is th
best-behaved of the youngsters. Alexander is timid and shy and she has little difficulty with
him. Arnold, on the other hand, is the dullest of the boys mentally and it is almost impossible
for him to concentrate. He is very easily led and gets into considerable difficulty and is spi
ful to her. She has discovered that Tony is the instigator of Arnold's actions and in order fo
the two boys to get along at all, she must separate them. She said she cannot trust Arnold to

32052-C   -19-

O'NEILL, Arnold

(With Mrs. ⸺ ⸺ . Cole Avenue, Pittsfield)B&C

8/31/54 knows whether he is coming for he is apt to wander all over town; stop on the way without any conception of time or orders. I asked her if both Alexander and his brother came home
together and why Alexander can't see that Arnold comes home with him, but she said Alexander is
very fearful of Arnold.

Anthony is sneaky and lies constantly. She said he is a boy who cannot be trusted. He is very
prone to take things; stealing not only from the house and school and grocery store, but from
anyone and anything. This was more prevalent—as well as the other difficulties—during the
school year, but not as much so during the summer.

I asked her what the boys had been doing during the vacation and she said that they have been
attending the movies once a week. We then talked about the meanings of transportation into town
and she said that occasionally she will drive them there, but, more often, in the nice weather
they walk and she denied that she will ever ride in the car concurrently while the boys are walking on the road. Her idea of an adequate vacation and leisure time activity for the boys is that
they play in the yard all day; go to the movies once a week; and she was very satisfied with the
fact that her husband takes them out for ice cream twice a week. Swimming is a thing of the
past. Since she nor any members of her family are able to swim, the boys do not go either. I
spoke to her about fall activities and suggested that they enroll at the Boy's Club and she said
that she had been thinking of this, too, and will apply for membership this year.

As for clothes, she said that the boys are always neat and clean when they leave the house. They
wear dungarees, as most of the boys at school do and change when they play afterwards. She said
that their clothes may not always be new after the children wear them for a while, but they are,
at least, clean. I spoke to her about the clothing allowance that is allotted for the boys. She
said that she had bought new outfits for them for school next week. She spoke about hand-me-
downs from one boy to another and I said that it would depend upon the condition of the clothes,
but even if there were few that could be used, the boys would also need their clothing allotment.
She said she cannot get everything at once because of the expense involved and I asked her if it
might not be possible for her to charge the clothes. She said that she would not do business th
way.

Regarding punishment, she said she finds it necessary very often to discipline them and in doing
so, she hollers at them and loses her temper with their behavior. When it is necessary, she
punishes them as she would her own children although with her children she was able to reason
with them and teach them right from wrong in this way. These boys, she said, are entirely different, and her teachings do not seem to penetrate. Since reasoning has proved unsuccessful, she
has, on occasion, sent them to bed. I asked her the length of their stay and she said, once or
twice it had been during a day, but sometimes it is during the morning when there is no school
and during the summer and not being able to play with the other youngsters is the worst punishment for them. I suggested that if it were necessary to punish the boys for their behavior,
they perhaps might be sent to bed an hour earlier. She told Worker that last week it was necessary to punish Arnold which she did by whipping his legs. She seems to feel that this whipping
or slapping would be done with her own children if it were necessary. I said that her treatmen
of her own children was something she and her husband decided, but that we would not condone or
approve of any whippings of a child under our care. * It is certainly not possible to deprive them of
any activities since they are so few in which they participate. I asked her why she never spoke
of punishment here — if she might she boys to bed at all without their meals. Also, she denied,
I tried to speak with her about the reasons that the boys might behave as they do and why they
might lie and be sneaky, but she seemed to completely disregard any motive behind their actions
She feels that this behavior is definitely a part of the boys and that they will never change,
but it might become worse as they get older. I went on to show her, and to further prove my poi
that little could be accomplished by these whippings and she agreed that she got no results fro
this punishment. This, however, seems to be her only way of attacking the problem.

I spoke with her about the added number of people in the family. When I mentioned about seeing

160

32052-C

O'NEIL, Arnold (P)

(With Mrs.   . _ ' Cole Avenue, Pittsfield) B&C

8/6/55 - (G. R. Earley) - Pl. Wi. Camp Russell, Richmond, Mass.   #72 to Summer camp.
Approved by RDC $18.00 week.   (bac)

8/21/55 - (G. R. Earley) Pl. with Mrs.   ..   _   . Cole Avenue, Pittsfield.
#79 Return to foster home from camp. Approved by RDC.   B&C   (bac)

1/6/55 - (G. R. Earley) Worker saw Arnold who just came in from school with a new coat. He
has recently received a p-jacket in addition. He briefly told the worker that he had a
pleasant Christmas then went upstairs to change. Foster mother said that his last physical
was June 1954.
                                                                          (MLG)
                                                                         1/13/56

1-20-55 - (G. R. Earley)   Worker made a school visit and talked to Miss   Miss   sa
that Arnold is quite a problem in the Redfield School. She realizes the deficiencies of
the foster mother. She said that last year a neighbor had left the milk money for the children but did not do so this year. He is apt to steal and arrives late at various times. Worker talked to Arnold whom Miss   . called into the office. He is extremely thin, however,
very submissive. When Miss ' _ asked him to read from his reading book, he did this reasonably well and she says that despite his inaptitude in arithmetic the boy loves to read. She
questions further as to whether he understands what he reads, but worker believes that he
must because he reads a good deal to himself. Arnold recently failed an eye examination.
                                                                          (MLG)
                                                                         1/13/56

2-25-55 - (G. R. Earley) Foster home visit, Arnold was being chastised and was sitting in a
chair in the kitchen. He seemed quite unhappy. Worker tried to explain to Mrs.   that
the boys should be encouraged to go to the Boys' Club as much as possible. He realizes that
Mrs. '   : will only do what she is required to do. and that only after considerable prodding.
No foster homes have been forthcoming. Worker believes that these children are known in the
community and are treated with kindness by the school authorities and the neighbors. Foster
father is kind to the boys and they have a certain amount of strength from the fact that they
are together and have been together for some time.
                                                                          (MLG)
                                                                         1/13/56

3-11-55 (G. R. Earley) Received clothing statment from Mrs.   . She spent only about one-
third of the clothing allowance this quarter.
                                                                          (MLG)

4-13-55 - (G. R. Earley) Worker received family supervision card this date.
                                                                          (MLG)
                                                                         1/13/56

4-19-55 - (G. R. Earley) Worker to the foster home.
                                                                          (MLG)
                                                                         1/13/56

*4/7/55 - (G. R. Earley) Worker learned while driving over to New York after Tony
who had run away that Arnold and the foster father are quite attached to each other. Arnold
sometimes goes over to Mr.   _n days which there are no school and spends the entire
day with him at the charcoal plant. According to Mrs. _. , foster father believes that
Arnold is the most likeable boy in the group. He seems to give Mrs.   . J considerable trouble,
however. She said that she believes that Arnold doesn't have sense enough to be afraid when
he should be. When worker tried to have her explain just what she meant by this she said
that he admits doing things brazenly which the other boys would be afraid to do.   (MLG)
                                                                         1/13/56

4-19-55 - (G. R. Earley) Foster home visit but Arnold was at the Boys' Club with the rest
of the foster children today. She says that he has an insatiable appetite. Worker mentioned
again the complaint that the children did not receive enough food. Mrs.   .. stoutly denied
this.
                                                                          (MLG)
                                                                         1/13/56

#32052

O'Neil, Arnold (P)

(Wi. Mrs.   Northampton St., Spfld.) (P) B&C #44612

11/25/57 - (C.N. s) number of months he and Vincent had been stealing. Arnold said that he was forced to steal in that Vincent threatened to beat him up if he didn't. I asked him why he didn't discuss this with me or foster parents and he could give me no reason. He was very shaken and repentant in his attitude concerning the thefts. He said that he associated with Vincent because he felt that he was a good boy. After they had begun stealing Arnold then tried to avoid him but was afraid.

Arnold was seen in Court by Judge   , who continued his case until January 6th, When it was explained that Arnold was being admitted to Belchertown State School. Judge expressed great sympathy for Arnold being led into this situation by Vincent and he warned Arnold to stay away from him. After the Court session Arnold and I talked again about the reasons for his getting into his past difficulty. I told him that we are going ahead with our plan to admit him to Belchertown State School. I explained in simple terms why it was necessary. He asked a number of questions about Belchertown. He wondered if the food was the same as he was getting now and also wondered what they did at the school at Christmas time. I told him that the food was good and that he would receive close and good supervision; it is doubtful whether he would be admitted to the school before Christmas but that the childre there enjoyed the same type of Christmas.

During our discussion Arnold said that he always tried to do the right thing but it always turned out to be wrong. I indicated that he would get the understanding and help that he needed at Belchertown. I also stated that his brother Alex and I would be visiting him regularly. Upon returning Arnold to his home, foster parents were informed of the Court appearance and of our intentions to go ahead with Arnold's admittance to Belchertown.
*   11/27/57 EHE

1/3/58 - (C.N. s) The completed descriptive application form and summary on Arnold forwarded to Belchertown State School today.   1/3/58 EHE

*1/2/58 - (C.N.(s) Letter from Belchertown State School stating that plans were being made to admit Arnold shortly. Custodial committment papers were enclosed for completion.
                                                                              1/3/58 EHE

1/2/58 - (C.N.   ) Visit to foster home to remind foster mother of Arnold's appearance in District Court on January 6th. It was also pointed out that since Arnold's application for committment to Belchertown State School is still pending, the case would probably be continued again.   1/15/57 EHE

1/6/58 - (C.N.   ) To foster home to pick up Arnold for his appearance in District Court today. Arnold was seen in Court by Judge   . Probation Officer   introduced the facts of the case to the Judge, with some additional information furnished by the Police Department. This new information indicated that Arnold had engaged in two stealing episodes since his last Court appearance. The instances involved the theft of another bicycle and a pair of motorcycle boots. In view of plans to have Arnold admitted to Belchertown State School, the Judge continued Arnold's case until January 27th. It was felt that Arnold would have been committed by this time, and thereby eliminate trial and disposition of this case.

Mr.   requested that he be notified when Arnold was committed. After returning Arnold home, foster mother discussed her desire to have Alex removed from the home as soon as possible. She revealed great disappointment in her experiences as a foster mother involving the placement and removal of Anthony   , Gary   and now Arnold and Alex O'Neil. She asked if, after the twins were removed, she couldn't have two younger but nice children placed in her home. She would like to prove to herself that she is an adequate person and

Gary Allen (Michael) Gaulin

DSR-1

-5-

33199-A

GAULIN, Gary Allen (P) (Called Michael)
(Wi. Mrs. ?   . Auburn St., Springfield)

10/3/47 - (BIB) Report of psychological examination received from Springfield Child Guidance clinic.   (JLF)

10/6/47 - (BIB) Wrote mother enclosing waiver for her to sign consenting to
adoption of child.   (JLF)

10/6/47 - (AMA) Approved and forwarded for payment bill of $5. from Dr.
for physical exam., for tbc test, and Hinton, negative.   (JCS)

10/14/47 - (BIB) Card returned from City Clerk, Division of Vital Statistics
Reno, Nevada, verifying marriage of :   .   .   . t
.   ... A certified copy may be obtained for one dollar.   (JLF)

10/20/47 - (BIB) Wrote Mrs. ?.   Child on free list from Nov. 1st on.
                                                                (JLF)

10/22/47 - (BIB) Ltr recd from Mrs.   .   stating she recd her certified
copy of marriage record and will keep it until it is needed for adoption
purposes.   (JLF)

3/12/48 - (AMF) AMA and AMF call at ' .   home. Family are out.
                                                                (JLF)

11/25/48 - (AMC) Pl. wi. House of Mercy Hospital, Pittsfield. Reason: In
auto accident wi. fos. mo.   (VEH)

12/11/48 - (AMC) Pl. wi. Mrs.   .   .   .   ., Richmond
Reason: Discharged from hospital. B&C.   (VEH)

1/6/49 - (AMC) Approved and forwarded bill of $152.50 from House of Mercy
Hospital, Pittsfield for board from 11/25 to 12/11 @ $6.00, $96.00; sutured
scalp and left hand and applied dressing on face, $10.00; anesthesia, $5.00
medications and oxygen, $31.50; x-ray of skull, $10.00. It is noted on the
bill that a credit of $104.00 is expected from Blue Cross.

1/6/49 - (AMC) Memo to AMF as follows: "I feel that we have no right to
allow Blue Cross to participate in this bill. If you feel the same way,
would you please drop the hospital a line?"   (VEH)

12/29/52 (J. H. Melville) Placed with Mrs.   . . Cole Avenue,
Pittsfield, Mass. (P) B&C Reason: Family moral condition.   (RSS)

******

33199-A   -7-

GAULIN, Gary Allen (P) (Called Michael)

(Wi. Mrs.   . Cole Avenue, Pittsfield) B & C

7/7/53 - (J.Melville) Visitor to '   . home, talked with boy alone and with
foster mother. Boy is youngest of four children placed in the home, is some-
what less shy than the other children, does not appear to be as scared of
Mrs.   as the others do. Boy was very excited when telling about seeing
Mrs.   .. at a mutual friend's home a few days previous to worker's visit.
He said that he liked it much better at the   ". . home than he did at the
        home. Said that he did not get enough to eat all the time, except when
Mr.   fed them, and that he liked Mr.   . very much, but did not care
for Mrs.   He appears to be in very good physical condition, plump, and
well-fed looking. He does not seem to play too well with the other children.
He is more inclined to stand off to one side. He seems somewhat moody and
commented on the fact that he had not been to church since being in the home
and had not been to a movie or had any real entertainment of any sort. He was
seen by Dr.   who happened to be at the home on another matter. He had
no comment to make on the boy's physical condition, which, as stated, appears
adequate.   (js)

7/24/53 - (J.Melville) Annual Physical Examination by Dr.   , Pitts.
Recommendations, none. Diagnosis: healthy normal child.   (js)

7/24/53 - (J.Melville) Worker to   home, talked with foster mother about
possibility of the children placed in her home going to summer camp. At this
time the Worker had in mind the   camp located in Williamstown. Worker had
checked with the Boys Club and found that at the present time they did not have
any openings, but they had promised to call if it were possible for the children
to go there this summer. Mrs.   stated that she thought two weeks or more
at camp would be very beneficial for the boys. Worker had thought there would'
be a little hostility to the idea and was surprised by her attitude, although
she stated that she did not feel that Tony   would benefit from camp. She
felt that he was a very bad influence on the boys and wondered if it were not
possible to send the other three children one week, and if Tony had to go at all
let him go by himself. She feels that Tony is behind most of the trouble that
she is having with the children. She feels quite strongly about it and even
asked that Tony be removed from her home. All four boys came in from playing
while Worker was there and Worker had a chance to talk with them for a short
time. All were in need of haircuts. Mrs.   ' manner of speaking to the boys
is pretty harsh at times. They seem to fear her.   (js)

Worker to Williamstown, talked with Mrs.   who operates the summer camp regarding the children who we plan to send to camp here. It was agreed that the
children will be sent within the next two weeks. Final date would be agreed on
later.   (js)

8/1/53 - (J.Melville) Worker received a call previous night from Mr.   at
the Boys Club in Pittsfield who stated that they would have room for the four
colored children, Tony Gregory, Alex and Arnold   and Gary, for the next
two weeks at Camp Russell Richmond and he wondered if boys could be ready to go
to camp on short notice, namely 1 day. He wanted them to go to camp Aug. 1-15.
Worker felt that in spite of the other arrangements which had been made to send
the boys to camp in Williamstown, this was a better opportunity. They would be
at a camp where there were much better physical resources, it would be a mixed
group and not a strictly colored one, and Worker felt that it would be good for
the boys to work into this type of a group if at all possible, inasmuch as in
their school work and after-hour play, they are continually with white children.

33199-A   -11-

GAULIN, Gary (Allen   P   (called Michael)

(wi. Mrs.   ., Pittsfield) B&C

Remarks: Cont. the home. As a result, the four children under the care of this
Division are sleeping in one-room in two double beds. This **is** over-crowded.
Anthony stated that they had never been beaten or mistreated at least for several months and he
felt that they had plenty to eat especially when -   ; was in charge of the meals. Another
complaint was the fact that the children are very much restricted to the area near their home;
although the playground is reasonably near, the children were not allowed to go down there.
Foster mother does not believe they will behave but she does not give them a chance to misbehave
because she does not allow them out of the yard. At this time, Worker was **ax** unable to talk to
foster mother who was on vacation. This is typical of her actions in leaving the care of the
children with her daughter and not notifying the Department. The **daughter** stated that she had
called Worker's home and was unable to reach **ikxxx** him. She did not write a note to the office.
                                                                                        (pk)

7/29/54 - (B. Ringer) Before the supervision of this case had been transferred to the present
worker, the former social worker had spoken with Fred   Superintendent of the Boys Bluc
of Pittsfield requesting that Gary be enrolled in the Boys Club Camp for the summer season.
On this day, letter received from Mr.   that due to unexpectedly large number of applicants
this year, the camp registration had been filled too early for the child to attend.   (VHS)

8/1/54 - (B. Ringer)   Case transferred to BER.

8/31/54 - (B. Ringer) Worker visited the   . home this day. (See foster home folder for information and investigation of recent complaints of the home and treatment of children - entries
dated 7/22/54 and 7/23/54.)

It was raining to-day and the boys were in the kitchen coloring and reading. Foster parents wer
with them. Worker had made an initial investigation of the home and after an introduction and
general conversation with the boys and foster parents, Mrs.   asked Worker into the other
room. She very quickly started in by saying that the boys were fine and that they had been having a very good summer. I told her, before we talked further, about the complaints that we had
recently received and that there had been several others since the former Worker had left. Although she was a little indignant, I did not detect any great surprise at what Worker said. She
said she could not understand why people said that the children were not getting enough to eat
since no one is in their home during mealtime and the family always eat together. She continued
on with the conversation, answering many statements as if she had anticipated what I was about
say. She said she is up in the morning and gives the boys a hot breakfast which she never did
for her own children. She said she is always here for lunch and their dinner includes fresh
vegetables from their garden. She repeated a number of times that she couldn't understand how
people could say that she was not at home constantly with the children. I told her that this
was not one of the complaints at all, but that it was the matter of the treatment that the chil
ren received, and I went on to enumerate the complaints. She admitted that she had sent them t
bed as a punishment several times without their meals, but that was only done in the beginning
and not of late.

Anthony, she said, has bus tickets which she allows him to use as he sees fit. However, he
occasionally walks to school with several of his friends and sells the tickets to buy ice cream
or candy. I asked her if Anthony took his lunch from the house and she said that he does this,
but then I questioned her about his milk which most of the children buy at school. She said
she was not able to give him money for a beverage because it is too expensive and if she did
give him money, she is sure that it would be spent on candy rather than on milk. The other
children, she said, have been coming home for lunch during the school time although they did
occasionally eat at school. In the afternoons the boys come home immediately after school. I
asked her if they played with any of the boys in the neighborhood. She said she doesn't want
them hanging around anywhere else because she is afraid that they will be very easily led and
that squabbles or difficulties will be blamed on these boys rather than on any other neighborhood boys. She said that the yard is large enough for them to play here and they can particip
in baseball and football games right in the yard. In addition, she said, there are swings and
-th-- -l--th'--- Th'- --mm-- she and Anthony worked in the vegetable garden. The boys have

33199-A   -13-

GAULIN, Gary Allen (called Michael) (P)

(With Mrs. .   . Cole Avenue, Pittsfield) (B&C)

8/31/54   They wear dungarees as most of the boys do at school and change when they play afterwards. She said that their clothes may not always be new after the children wear them for a whi
but they are, at least, clean. I spoke to her about the clothing allowance that is allotted for
the boys. She said that she had bought new outfits for them for school next week. She spoke
about hand-me-downs from one boy to another and I said that it would depend upon the condition o
the clothes, but even if there were a few that could be used, the boys also need their full clot
ing allotment. She said she cannot get everything at once because of the expense involved and
I asked her if it might not be possible for her to charge the clothes. She said that she would
not do business that way.

Regarding punishment, she said she finds it necessary very often to discipline them and in doing
so, she hollers at them and loses her temper with their behavior. When it is necessary she
punishes them as she would her own children although with her children she was able to reason
with them and teach them right from wrong in this way. These boys, she said, are entirely diffe
ent, and her teachings do not seem to penetrate. Since reasoning has proved unsuccessful, she
has, on occasion, sent them to bed. I asked her the length of their stay and she said once or
twice it had been during a day, but sometimes it is during the morning when there is no school
and during the summer and not being able to play with the other youngsters is the worst punishmen
for them. I suggested that if it were necessary to punish the boys for their behavior, they perhaps might be sent to bed an hour earlier.* She told Worker that last week it was necessary to
punish Arnold which she did by whipping his legs.   She seems to feel that this whipping or
slapping would be done with her own children if it were necessary. I said that her treatment of
her own children was something she and her husband could decide, but that we would not condone o
approve of any whippings of a child under our care. I tried to speak with her about the reasons
that the boys might behave as they do and I think might lie and be sneaky, but she seemed to completely disregard any motive behind their actions. She feels that this behavior is definitely
a part of the boys and that they will never change, but it might become worse as they get older.
* It is certainly not possible to deprive them of an activity are are not in in their they participate. I make too not
in the form of punishment have — if they feel then & tel it all without their much. This, she desire.
I went on to tow her, and to further prove my point, that little could be accomplished by these
whippings and she agreed that she got no results from this punishment. This, however, seems to
be her only way of attacking the problem.

I spoke with her about the added number of people in the family. When I mentioned about seeing
the sleeping arrangements, she was extremely dubious in showing me the upstairs rooms. She ver
quickly said that two boys sleep in one room and two in the other. There are five bedrooms upstairs and one on the first floor, the latter which she uses. One bedroom upstairs is occupied
by her daughter and grandchild; the second room by her son, daughter-in-law and grandchild; the
third by two foster children; the fourth by two other foster children; and the fifth is used by
her husband when he sleeps days and works nights and in the evenings her son sleeps in the room.
I asked her what arrangements were made when her husband is on vacation or has a day off and she
claims that he sleeps in the downstairs bedroom. I told Mrs. .   . again that I would like to
see the rooms and when we went upstairs, she pointed out a room containing a cot, bureau and
chair which, she said, is used by Anthony. The second bedroom used by the foster children con-
tained two double beds and she said that this is used by the other three boys. When I spoke wit
her about her statement previously when she had told me that they sleep two in one room and two
in the other, she very quickly reversed her statement, saying that she "thought she had mentione
that three sleep in one room and Tony has a room of his own." Seeing two double beds, Worker is
of the belief that all four boys sleep in one room and this was corroborated in a former dicta-
tion.

In the boys' room, I noticed a Department suitcase filled with clothes and I asked her why the
clothes were not put in bureau drawers. Her reason was that the boys had expected to go to camp
the first two weeks in August and they had packed in preparation. I asked her why the clothes
had not been put away since it was now three weeks from their anticipated departure and I also
spoke with her about the letter that we had received, saying that there was not enough room at
camp for the boys to attend this year.

33199- A   (18)

GAULIN, Gary Allen   (Called Michael) (P)

(With Mrs. ~~Harriet Frances Gaulin discussed Rittafiels~~) (B&C)
                                    Northampton St., Springfield)

1-15-57 - (G. R. Earley) Continued. an adult boarder but they were too much trouble.
Worker has given Mrs.   the benefit of every doubt. Refer to O'Neil history and
to Anthony Gregory's history for additional information.   (MLG) 4-4-57

1-16-57 - (G. R. Earley) Worker drove the boys into Springfield after picking up transfer
cards. They seemed in good spirits and worker explained to them as he had several times
in front of Mrs..,   that they deserve more kindness and attention than to live with
a woman with a better disposition.   Upon arrival at the   home in Springfield, the
children immediately had lunch. Worker had previously explained to Mrs.   and she
had been willing to take all four children. A copy of Gary's report card was as follows:
Language S; Social Studies S; Arithmetic S; Science S; Art S; Music S; Physical Education
S; Conduct S; Work Habits S; Getting along with other pupils, S;   (MLG) 4-4-57

1-28-57 - (G. R. Earley) Worker received call from Miss   , School Adjustment
Counsellor, regarding plans for testing. She will let us know. Gary is attending the
Homer School.   (MLG) 4-4-57

1-29-57 - (G. R. Earley) To   for Anthony and Alexander. Mrs.   appears
to like Gary.   (MLG) 4-4-57

*10-24-56 - (G. R. Earley) Worker to Pittsfield General Hospital then to Mrs.
She said that the School nurse was there yesterday and that the school doctor would not
recommend that Mike has his tonsils taken out.

Worker said that the examination at the hospital clinic would be the deciding factor. Mrs.
        said that Michael is a fine little boy. He is bright in school, clean personally and
in her opinion could go on to higher education. He attends the Baptist Church with the
other boys. She asked worker if we would reimburse her for Cod Liver Oil which the doctor
recommended. He needs it four times a day during the winter.   (MLG) 4-4-57

*11-6-56 - (G. R. Earley) Worker to Mrs.   , a neighbor, then Mrs.   regarding
Anthony Gregory (See latter's record)   (MLG) 4-4-57

*11-20-56 - (G. R. Earley) To foster home; Mrs.   was there but the boys were at the
Boys' Club.   (MLG) 4-4-57

2-12-57 - (G. R. Earley) Telephone call to Mr..   regarding Arnold   He had to
talk sharply to the boys one night to make them go to bed early.   (MLG) 4-4-57

2-21-57 - (G. R. Earley) Foster home visit; Gary scheduled for testing for March by
the School Department which is their policy for children entering their school system.
                                                                (MLG) 4-4-57

3-18-57 - (G. R. Earley) Mrs.   is having difficulty with Arnold   but she
says that she gets good results with "Mike" or Gary as she calls him.   (MLG) 4-4-57

4-4-57 - (G. R. Earley) Telephone call from Mr. Weldon of the Y.M.C.A. at Camp Norwich.
He plans to accept applications from the boys.   (MLG) 4-4-57

4/8/57 - (G.R. Earley) Worker to Mr. and Mrs.   Gary was present. Mrs.
is being concerned about the fact that Gary is taking things form the neighbors. Gary impressed the worker as not being a happy boy. This impression was first learned last Fall
while Gary was still in the   home in Pittsfield, and his attitude does not seem to
have changed. It appears that Gary has an attitude of £ I'm going to get what I can out
of things". He seems to have almost a hard-boiled attitude. Mr. and Mrs.

33199-A

GAULIN, Gary Allan (Called Michael) (P)

(Wi. M_{rs.}　　　　　　　Northampton St., Spfld) B&C

4/8/57 - (GRE) cont. - feel as though they can handle him but whether they can really understand him or give the boy the affection he needs, is another matter. 4/24/57 (bac)

4/22/57 - (G.R. Earley) Mrs.　　　i to the office along with Tony　　　She said that Gary stole something over $15. from a neighbor and she is worried about it. She said that he needs help, posibly psychiatric help and she is taking the children for their examination to a doctor and will ask him to especially watch Gary. Subject of this visit was primarily Tony Gregory who is accused by M_rs.　　　　of staying too long at neighbors homes, and she was requesting his removal.　　　4/24/57　(bac)

5/2/57 (F.Donaldson) Worker accompanying fellow worker, J. Donahue to the home of Mrs.
　　　, Northampton Ave., Springfield, as Mr. Donohue had no means of transportation and interviewed Mrs.　　　During the visit Mr. Donahue interviewed Tony and Mrs.　　　privately and then stepped out to talk with Mrs.　　　, referring to the matter of Mike's (Gary's) stealing which Mrs.　　　raised to worker. Tony, Alexander and Arnold were in the room with Mike and worker and had been present when the matter of Mike's stealing was mentioned and also had been involved as receivers of portions of the money that Mike Stole. Worker asked Mike if he could give any reason for stealing. He couldn't. Worker asked if he was disatisfied with his present home or if he had any trouble in the home or at school. Mike said he had no troubles and got along well at home and at school. Worker asked if he wanted something he did not have and he said "No". At this point Tony volunteered that Mike wanted a bike and a watch. Mrs.　　　had said that Mike had taken a watch but that it had by now been returned. Worker asked if Mike had talked about his wants with the
　　　and Mike said "No". He didn't know why he had not done so. Worker asked if he had been in the habit of taking things that did not belong to him. At this point Tony, Alexander and Arnold all stated that at the previous home, Mrs.　　　' home, they had all been in the habit of taking whatever was around whenever possible - they had to get anything. Worker asked if they all still did the same thing. They said "No, they didn't have to here because they got what they needed". They said that Mike was the only one who had not stopped stealing. Worker suggested to Mike that he tell Mrs.　　　of his desires and explained that if Mrs.　　　knew their wants, there would be a better chance of working out a solution.
　　　　　　　　　　　　　(EM) 5/7/57.

6/10/57 - (M.Shea) Medical examination report received this date from Dr. Nelson Newmark. Diagnosis: Normal boy. Recommendations: Should be seen at Child Guidance Clinic because he tends to steal.　　　6/24/57　(LGB)

6/19/57 - (C.N.Gibbs) During Worker's visit at the home of Mr. & Mrs.　　　to discuss their decision to have Tony removed from the home, Worker was informed by Mr.　　　that Mike had been involved in the theft of two (2) watches. These watches have subsequently been found and returned to the owners. Mr. & Mrs.　　　evidenced great concern about Mike's stealing. They also complained that Arnold　　　another foster child in the home, was spreading information about Mike's stealing throughout the neighborhood.　　 7/3/57　EHE

7/1/57 - (C.N.Gibbs) Worker to Highland Branch YMCA, 171 Eastern Ave. to see George Executive Secretary to arrange for Arnold and Alec　　　and Gary Gaulin to attend Day Camp. Mr.　　　stated that boys would be allowed to attend Day Camp and that there are funds available for Camperships. Worker advised that boys will be able to start Tuesday July 2nd.
　　　　　　　　　　　　7/11/57　EHE

7/27/57 - (C. Gibbs)　TO: Springfield Boy's Club Camp, Brimfield, Mass
#72 Camp Placement　　　APPROVED: RDC.　　To Bill
　　　　　　　　　　　　　　　　　　　　　(mr)

Alexander Robert O'Neil

-13

32052-B

O'NEILL, Alexander

(Wl. Mrs   , Ave., Pittsfield)

2/12/54 - (J. Melville) Worker to home, left some clothing for Alex and
Arnold which had been given to Worker by another foster mother. Clothing
was in very good repair and it worked out very nicely with the O'Neil twins.
Foster mother has been somewhat difficult regarding clothing. She does not
spend anywhere near the boys' normal allowance, as a result the children
are poorly clothed and do not make their best appearance. Foster mother
appears to be very fond of Arnold, stated she did not receive any more poor
reports from school on the two children. She was somewhat disturbed by
the manners of both children, said that Alex in particular had some very
bad habits when outside the home. Had observed him on several occasions
going into neighbors' yards and taking things from their garbage pails. Worker
questioned whether the boy is really getting enough to eat in this home. She
assured Worker that boy was, could not understand the reason for his actions.
She is somewhat disappointed in the children.

3/26/54 - (J. Melville) Worker to the home and talked with foster mother and
with Arnold who evidently has been saving his papers for a considerable
period of time and they are all marked A or B, although a quick glance at
some of the papers show that the mark given was probably given for encourage-
ment only as the work was very substandard. Alex appears to be doing slightly
better than Arnold. During visits to the school, teacher seems to be more
concerned about Arnold than his brother.   (ES)

Worker has been somewhat disturbed by continuing difficulty with this home.
There are so many poor points to be found that continued use of the home
seems rather futile. Foster mother is very uncooperative, refuses to accept
supervision and if pressed about matters of policies becomes very argumentive
and difficult. It took almost one year and one-half of constant prodding
before she would take four children for an annual physical. Worker has never
been able to get her to provide the children with milk at a noon day meal
which they have at school. The lunches which the children take vary between
bearly adequate and insufficient. During recent physical examination all
four children needed vitamins and treatment for one condition or another.
Worker discussed these things with her today, but Worker got the impression
it would be another struggle to get foster mother to carry out the various
requests. The home is being used because of a lack of another 'colored' foster
home facility. If she were willing to cooperate this could be an excellent
home because the physical appearances are exceptional. Worker believes that
the situation will get worse when Mrs.   ' two boys come home from the
service. Worker has heard very poor reports of their behavior when in the
Pittsfield School System and is not looking forward to their returning to
the home.   (ES)

5/4/54 - (J. Melville) Worker to Redfield School, talked with Principal and later
talked with both boys alone at great length. Worker talked with them chiefly
regarding conditions in their foster home, their treatment, meals they received and whether or not there was any mistreatment, by foster mother
and for the most part boys replied in the negative. They appear to be
fairly happy here and made no real complaints, but perhaps they just do not
realize the difference between good and bad treatment. Both of them are
looking forward to going to camp again this summer. This was their chief
topic of conversation and they usually talked the conversation back to this

(2:

32052

O'NEIL, Alexander (P)
Northampton St., Springfield) B&C
(With Mrs. ~~XXXXXXXXXXXXXXXXXXXXXXXXXXXXXXXXXXX~~) B&C

11-7-56 - (G. R. Earley) Worker to Miss Bertuli's and then to Mrs.
(MLG) 4-4-57

11-20-56 - (G. R. Earley) To foster home; Mrs.   was at home alone. The boys were at
the Boys' Club. She said that they have obtained good report card. (MLG) 4-4-57

12-12-56 - (G. R. Earley) Dental estimate received. (MLG) 4-4-57

12-17-56 - (G. R. Earley) Letter from Plunkett School, Principal, requesting the visitor to
see him. (MLG) 4-4-57

12-19-56 (G. R. Earley) Worker to the Plunkett School and talked with the PRincipal, Mr.
Alexander is doing better then Arnold. He heard that all the children were stealing
from shops on North Street. Worker said that he had been looking for a long time for a new
foster home for them, and that there was one which was a prospect. (MLG) 4-4-57

1-15-57 - (G. R Earley) Worker to Mrs.   regarding moving of the children to Springfield
(MLG) 4-4-57

1-16-57 - (G. R. Earley) Worker moved all four children into Springfield to the
home. (MLG) 4-4-57

1/30/57 - (G.R. Earley) Worker to   home to bring Alex and Arnold to the Child
Guidance Clinic for psychometric. Both boys were in good spirits, claimed to like Mr. and
Mrs.   quite a bit. Arnold especially said that they treated the children much
nicer than Mrs.   had. While at the Clinic, Arnold behaved very well and Mrs.
had a favorable impression of the boy. Worker explained to her that Arnold would "push"
for everything that he could get away with but that if he was treated with a firm but kind
hand, better things could be expected of him than what perhaps the psychometric would indi-
cate. For this reason, Mrs.   is going to try and enroll Arnold at a school with a
male teacher. After the testing, worker and the two boys walked back to   s having
an ice cream on the way. Alex was much more outgoing than previously and Arnold of course,
is always in good spirits. To date, this placement appears to be going well. 4/17/57 (bac)

2/21/57 - (G.R. Earley) Foster home visit while the children were at school. Mrs.
has a good deal of patience with the children being almost too easy if anything. Mr.
is relied upon for correcting them since he works alternating shifts, he is not always
at home at the times when the children are home in the evening. Mrs.   on a couple
of occasions had difficulty in getting them to quiet down before going to sleep at night.
4/17/57   (bac)

3/18/57 - (G.R. Earley) Foster home visit. This visit was primarily concerned with Tony
and Arnold   Foster mother realizes that Alex is more intelligent than
Arnold and takes better care of his clothing. 4/17/57 (bac)

4/4/57 - (G.R. Earley) Worker received telephone call from Mr.   of the YMCA, Camp
Norwich regarding plans for four boys in the   home to attend summer camp, at a
time to coincide with the foster parents two weeks vacation. Worker approved of the camp
application and said that he would have to work out details later regarding expense.
4/17/57 (bac)

4/8/57 (G.R. Earley) Worker to M.   and M.

170

#32052-B

O'NEIL, Alexander   (P)

(With Mrs.   Pendleton Ave., Springfield) B&C
          #45344   (P)

10/20/60 - (A.B. Coville) Cont'd.   some of the schoolmates. It seemed his lunch
had been stolen that very day. Because of Alex's shyness and physical frailness he is subjec
to some bullying by certain of his fellow pupils.

In Alex's opinion and he spoke more determinely of this than anything else, foster parents'
9 p.m. curfew has restricted him socially and become a sore point with him. He said he had
been embarrassed by their calling the homes of some of his friends on certain nights when he
didn't make it home by 9 o'clock. This plus the fact that "he never has money" recently cost
him his girlfriend. I asked Alex if he had thought of looking for a job after school, nights
to make himself extra spending money and he replied that he had had a job at Pennys Departmen
Store but failed to show up for work one night during his first week of work and was similarl
fired. He had not looked for another job since then because he just didn't think he could ge
one.

There is obviously no love lost between Alex and foster father and suggestions that he be
removed from this home, which had previously been clearly hinted at by foster parents in pass
have now become practical demands.   11/29/60 (L

1/11/61 - (A.B. Coville) We had been under constant urging from foster mother for the past
month to remove Alex from her home because of a situation which appears to have developed because of a personality clash between Alex and his foster father. Foster mother fears that if
Alex, whose apathetic attitude is getting under foster father's skin, is allowed to remain in
the home much longer foster father in a moment of weakness might use harsh physical disciplin
on him.

Foster mother had called the office the previous day and informed me that she had been notifi
by the school authorities at Trade High that Alex was failing two subjects and in jeopardy.
Because of this I visited Trade High today and spoke with Mr.   , Student Adjustment
Counsellor for tenth grade students. Mr.   was not too familiar with Alex but assurec
me the notice that foster mother had received was merely a form letter designed to stir up a
little reaction in parents which reaction may have an efficacious effect on their child's
school efforts. I spoke with Mr.   , Alex's mathematics teacher. Math is one of the
subjects which Alex received a failing mark in and Mr.   , who was surprisingly generous
in his appraisal of the boy, stated that Alex was certainly not failing through any lack of
effort, that he was an honest student and in his opinion was making a maximum effort to master
his studies. However, his math deficiency seems to be a matter of inadequate background.
Last year at Buckingham Junior High School Alex had just barely passed eighth grade math and
was now being forced to take tenth grade math. Mr.   did not seem the least bit doubtfu
that Alex would eventually right himself and pass the course, and he and Mr.   both
assured me that the boy was in no danger of being expelled from school. Their comments of
Alex's personality, general attitude, and application were in marked contrast to the appraises
of him that we have received from his foster parents in recent months. Mr.   also
observes that because of the character of the curriculum and personal traits that he felt
peculiar to Trade High's schedule that it was possible for a reticient, unaggressive boy such
as Alex to become lost in the shuffle at Trade if he refused to assert himself, or otherwise
draw himself to the attention of his teachers and he would not eliminate the possibility that
Alex could be going to the wrong high school.   1/17/61 (IA)

6/14/61 (C.C.Dugan) - Letter to foster mother enclosing small snapshot of Alex's brother who
had visited the office on 6/13 and spoke with Mr. Scully. Advised mother to have Alex stay
near the house Sat., 6/17/61 as Alex's brother, Charles, plans to come up from Boston
that day to see him as he was unable to see him on 6/13/61.   (em) 6/14/61

#32052-B

O'NEIL, Alexander   (P)

(With Mrs. _____ ., Pendleton Ave., Springfield) B&C
      #45344   (P)

6-15-61 - (A. Coville) Charles O'Neil appeared at Springfield District Office today requesting information as to the whereabouts of Alex and Alex's twin brother, Arnold. This worker
was not in the office at the time and Charles spoke with Mr. Scully. Charles has recently
been discharged by the Youth Service Board, and is currently living in Boston and working in
that city. He had not seen Alex in quite a number of years, and Mr. Scully provided him wit
the address of Alex's foster home.   6-20-61 (IA)

6-19-61 - (A. Coville)   Mrs. Dorothy _____ of 29 Stebbin Street, Springfield, came to the
office this morning and identified herself as Alex's maternal aunt. She expressed some
indignation at the fact that Alex had been allowed to lose contact so completely with member
of his family, and said that both she and her mother, Mrs. Ann ____ who lives upstairs fr
her at Stebbin St. address, are both interested in providing a home for Alex, and in fact
wish also to provide a home for Arnold, who is presently at the State School in Belchertown.
Worker asked Mrs. ____ if she, or any of her kin folks, had ever contacted D.C.G. in the
past to obtain information about Alex and his brother. She replied somewhat vaguely that sh
had a couple of years ago, but had been given the "run around." She said that she had bumpe
into Charles O'Neil on the street Friday and he had looked familiar to her, and she asked hi
his name, when he replied she identified herself to him as his aunt. She said he had brough
Alex to visit her Friday and Alex had been back both Saturday and Sunday to visit.

Mrs. ____ is a woman of 40 years, is legally separated from her husband and lives with her
five daughters, ages 5, 8, 11, 14, and 17. Mrs. ____ volunteered that she receives an ADC
Grant for herself and her five children.

Mrs. ____ mother, Mrs. Ann ____, is 63 years of age. She lives with her husband, Mr.
____, who is employed by the City of Springfield. They have two sons, 18 and 19 years old
living with them and both currently unemployed.

I indicated to Mrs. ____ that this Division would gladly take into consideration their
request to have Alex placed with either her or her mother, and by way of preliminary investigation, promised to see both parties later on in the week.

Later that day I talked with Alex at his foster home. He said he had been very glad to meet
his newly found relatives, and he was anxious to move in with them. He said he knew the
____ boys before, but was unaware they were his uncles. Alex said that he has a small
job lined up with the Hathaway Tobbacco Company; said that though the issue had been somewhat
doubtful, he had passed his freshman year at Trade High and definitely wants to continue next
year. Alex's reaction to the mention of his foster father was that he is still having some
difficulty in getting along with that gentleman, and he said that he hoped that if he were
moving to live with relatives, that it would be effective as soon as possible. I assured him
that it would be.   6-20-61 (IA)

7-14-61 - (A. Coville) Visited foster home and Alex was helping foster father repair the
front stairs of the house. Relationship between the two seems something quite less than
cordial. Foster father constantly incurs harsh demands on Alex. Alex is professing to be
very anxious to go to live with his grandmother. He is a taciturn, docile boy and doesn't
express himself strongly, talking constantly in a low voice. I told Alex that his move to hi
grandmother's was pending merely the return of a couple of references which grandmother had
given. Alex has this week off from tobacco farm.

7-14-61 - (A. Coville) Talked with maternal grandmother, Mrs. Anne ____, at her home at
____ Stebbins Street today. Mrs. ____ has been growing a little impatient with the process

#32052-B

O'NEIL, Alexander   (P)

(With Mrs.   Pendleton Ave., Springfield) B&C
#45344   (P)

8-2-61 - (A. Coville) Continued:

Mrs. Anne   9 Stebbins Street, Springfield. This
woman is Alexander's maternal grandmother. She had been
out of touch with Alexander and his brothers for some
number of years, and now was professing great interest in
having them, or at least Alexander, come to live with her.

A home evaluation was initiated with favorable records, and
Alexander was discharged to the custody of his grandmother on
8-2-61. Grandmother indicating that she would immediately
apply for ADC.

8-8-61 (IA)

8/2/61 - (A.Coville) TO: MRS. ANNE .   Stebbins Street, Springfield
#89 DISCHARGED TO GRANDMOTHER ON ADC   APPROVED: LFS   (mr

5/10/66 (MTSullivan) Letter from Alexander now in Okinowa with the Marine Corps, enclosing

a Statement of Peersonal History Form which has to be completed for top secret clearance.
Completed the schools and grades Alexander attended and gave a list of his foster home address
Alexander's address is L/Cpl A. R. O'Neil, Box M.B., U.SWAF, F.P.O., San Francisco,Calif. (s

#32052-B

O'NEIL, Alexander   (P)

(With Mrs.   Pendleton Ave., Springfield) B&C
    #45344   (P)

7-14-61 - (A. Coville) (Cont'd.)   holdup was merely a matter of our waiting for her or reference to reply, and I explained that this was a necessary procedure in a case of this type; that the stumbling block so far has been obtaining the reference of Clergyman, Reverend Fullilove, but when she approached the Reverend for a reference he had said that he had been out of contact with the family for so long that he could not in conscience act as a reference for them at this time. There is another church in the neighborhood, the pastor of which Mrs. has been thinking of approaching for a reference, and I urged her to make herself known to this man in order to enable him to make any investigation he might want to make before recommending or refusing her, and she indicated that she would attempt to make contact with this man the following day. Grandmother leaves no doubt that she is extremely anxious for Alex to come to live with her.   7-18-61 (IA)

8-2-61 - (A. Coville) Worker talked with Alex today in the foster home. I was in the home when he returned from work. He is still employed on a summer job at a tobacco farm in Suffolk. I informed Alex that final arrangements had been completed prior to his going to live with his grandmother. I told him that I had just spoken with grandmother and foster parents, and if he wished he could make the move this evening. His grandmother's home is only a matter of several blocks from the foster home. Alex was happy to hear this news. Foster parents had displayed practically no emotion at Alex's impending move.

We had been aware that boy had not been completely happy in this home, nor were foster parents overly pleased with him. However, in talking with Alex privately today, he said that he was happy to be going to live with his grandmother primarily because she was a relative, and having relatives who care for him is still a very novel idea to Alex. Unsolicitously, he told me that he had nothing against the .   said he had been in several foster homes and considered their home by far the best in which he has lived.

We talked about his future schooling, and he verbalized real determination to finish school. He has two more years to go at Trade High.

It was nearly supper time and foster mother wanted Alex to have his supper with them and then offered to transport him and his clothing to his grandmother's this evening.   8-8-61 (IA)

8-2-61 - (A. Coville)

DISCHARGE SUMMARY: Alexander O'Neil was received into the care of D.C.G. on 2-6-45 along with his twin brother Arnold. At the time, his older brother, Charles, was already with D.C.G. In November of 1951, brother Charles, nine years of age at the time, was discharged to the Youth Service Board; and in January of 1958 Alexander's twin brother, Arnold, was discharged to Belchertown State School.

During his sixteen years with the D.C.G., Alexander was in several foster home placements. His last foster home placement being some three and one-half years in duration. Alexander has always been a quiet, retiring boy, and these traits may have hampered his home adjustments. His foster home placements were not marked by noticeable incident; were apparently not happy experiences for the boy.

Anthony H. Gregory

Anthony Gregory's D.S.S. files were unobtainable due to the Massachusetts privacy laws regarding deceased wards of the state.

EPILOGUE

Writing this book was not easy. The idea to write it had been in the back of my mind for a long time but I would always find excuses not to write it. After talking with my two brothers, Arnold and Michael, and some close friends, I decided to go ahead and write. The memories of the pain and suffering that we endured rushed back into my mind just as if it had happened yesterday. Surely there will be those that will read this book and hate my guts; others may be a little embarrassed. On the other hand, there will be those that will love me for it and commend me. I wrote this book for all of the children that are still in foster homes and forgotten.

In the early years it was hard to find a foster home, especially a colored one. When one was found, the Department of Child Guidance cut corners in order to have the child placed. Some of the standards that were set were overlooked. Background checks on potential foster parents were limited. Visits to the homes were few and far between. Complaints were swept under the rug.

There were a large number of deficiencies that plagued the D.C.G. Poorly trained and unsupervised workers; a lack of long-term planning for and monitoring of children in state custody; a lack of due process and careful case review by the courts in handling children's cases; a tendency to institutionalize children in lieu of preferable community-based options; a lack of case responsibility as clients were transferred from local area workers to other workers at other levels in the agency; and last but not least, an overburdening of social workers with excessive case loads.

For many years there had been recurring criticism of the public services for children as being fragmented, inefficient, and ineffective. Responsibility for services was divided among six or more state agencies. Major responsibility for dependent and neglected children resided in the Department of Public Welfare, where social service functions were constantly being overwhelmed by the pressures of income maintenance programs.

The creation of a new Department of Social Services in 1972 marked a significant turning point in the organization of services for children in Massachusetts. It was the product of developments extending over a period of ten years or more.

It is a known fact that there are still foster children in homes suffering at the hands of brutal foster parents. Sometimes the Department of Social Services is overburdened and unable to dedicate the time, energy, and manpower to completely and thoroughly investigate the spiraling number of caseloads that flood the department. Consequently, proverbial cracks develop within the system and children fall through them, becoming the victims of everlasting effects.

There are a lot of children that will need a loving home. Finding one is not an easy task. There are a lot of good foster homes out there filled with love and understanding, something that those children need.

Today, the Division of Social Services (D.S.S.) has what is known as 51-a forms, which basically are reports of child abuse and neglect. These reports are made from law enforcement personnel, doctors and hospital personnel, school teachers, family members, or concerned citizens that may have knowledge of child abuse or neglect. Once the report is made, D.S.S. does a vigorous follow-up investigation. The social worker will go to the school and talk with the child in question as well as their teachers regarding to any signs of changes in a child's behavior. They also conduct what is referred to as a home study, actually going to the foster home and interviewing the foster parents regarding the allegations. They still have limited resources to work with, but a whole lot more than they had in 1952!

In any event I sincerely hope that this book will help those children that are still "down back"

"THE FOUR BOYS"

Tony

Anthony "Henry" Gregory—In 1959 Tony enlisted in the Marines. He served two years and was discharged because of his refusal to conform to military standards. He married and raised four children.

Unfortunately, his marriage ended and he started hanging out with the wrong people, drinking and constantly getting into trouble with the law. It seemed as though Tony just gave up on life.

In March of 1985, Tony died of cancer. He was forty-four years old. I guess he finally found peace at last. Right now he is probably playing cowboys and Indians with the angels. I miss him, "the bossy cow."

Arnold

Arnold Barry O' Neil—In 1958 Arnold was placed in the Belchertown State School in Belchertown, Massachusetts, by the Department of Child Guardianship. They felt that he was too incompetent to be placed in another foster home.

During the time that Arnold was in the school, he was repeatedly beaten by staff members of the school. They would go to his room and take him into a bathroom, then toss a coin to see which one would do the beating, using an aluminum baseball bat. Other times they would punch him in the face and stomach with their hands as though he was an adult. One staff member befriended him gave him a guitar to play, which he learned to play very well.

Charles visited Arnold a couple of times while he was in the state school, and during those visits he told Arnold about his family. This made Arnold more determined to get out of the institution.

April 4, 1962, Arnold managed to get out of the Belchertown State School with the aid of the staff member that gave him the guitar. Once he got out he hopped a train to Enfield, Connecticut. From there he hitchhiked to Dorchester, Massachusetts. He located his brother Charles. Both of them spent a lot of time together getting to know one another.

Charles took Arnold to Springfield to meet his biological family. Upon meeting his family Arnold displayed a lot of hostility towards them. He felt that they had abandoned him at childhood and that they did nothing to have him removed from the Belchertown State School.

It took Arnold some time to adjust to life with those memories bottled up inside him. He married and has two children. His marriage ended and he left Massachusetts, moving out to the Midwest. Arnold excelled in country music and performed in a number of well-known venues, such as the Nashville Music Theater, under the stage name Neil Arnold. He is deeply involved with a beautiful African girl name Ruby and plans to marry her soon. He is a security officer for numerous housing complexes in Colorado.

Arnold has put the past behind him and is leading a productive life. He now resides in Aurora, Colorado.

Michael

Gary Allen (Michael) Gaulin—"Big Head" Michael enlisted in the Marines in 1963 and did a hitch in Vietnam. He was honorably discharged in 1966 and settled down in Springfield, Massachusetts. Michael worked as a security officer at a local hospital for a number of years. Unfortunately, a patient caught him on one of his bad days and hit him in the face. Consequently, Michael "lost it" and hit the patient back. That caused him to lose his job. He now works for a trucking company doing delivery service.

Michael is an avid fisherman. Fishing is his life; there is not a day that goes by that you won't find Michael on a bank or in a boat doing his thing. After work, Michael was always the quiet one and always kept to himself.

Michael has tried to find out what happened to his family but as of yet he has been unable to obtain any information on his biological parents. Maybe someday he will find what he is looking for and hopefully have the peace of mind that he deserves.

He is married (currently separated), has three children, and resides in West Springfield, Massachusetts.

On a sunny afternoon in October 2004, Gary A. Gaulin (Michael) met with his biological family for the first time. Through an intensive search of hospital and D.S.S. documents, he discovered that he in fact did have biological relatives living in Springfield, Massachusetts. Plans were made to meet with them. In doing so, he found out what actually happened to him at birth and who his parents were. He learned that his mother passed away in 1996 and is buried in Chicopee, Massachusetts.

Michael now has peace of mind.

About the Author

Alexander Robert O'Neil spent the first sixteen years of his life in foster care being shuffled from one home to another. In 1961 he was removed from the Massachusetts State welfare system and placed with his biological relatives in Springfield, Massachusetts. In 1963 he enlisted in the Marines, serving four years including a tour in Vietnam. Upon his discharge in 1967 he settled down in Springfield, Massachusetts, working odd jobs and just "hanging around." In 1973 he joined the Springfield Police Department and is currently assigned to the Detective Bureau Burglary Squad. He has three children.

Printed in the United States
202546BV00001B/196-300/A